My Wo[

Fran

The Biography of an amazing girl, by Paul Spelzini.

This book is dedicated to the memory of the late Francesca Laura Spelzini. R.I.P. An utterly amazing person who was too good for this world and was an inspiration to all those who knew her.

[Cover picture taken on Mount Moraine, Canada; August 2006]

Preface;

This is a true life story about my late daughter, Francesca Laura Spelzini, who was born on the 19th April 1991 and sadly died on June 30th 2009. More importantly perhaps, this is also a story about her fight against complications with mental illness which she ultimately lost, but not without one hell of a fight and sheer determination to complete her studies and leave her mark on this world with a lasting legacy.

Prior to her birth, we were just an ordinary young suburban family with 2 little boys living in Southgate, North London before moving to St. Albans to embark on an 18 year emotional rollercoaster ride we couldn't have even begun to have imagined.

Since her death, we have reverted to normality, if we can ever be 'normal' or genuinely happy ever again. But in the 18 years Francesca was part of our family, she took us to places we didn't even know existed physically and emotionally. We also learned a great deal about Asperger's Syndrome and all of its complications, as I suspect it runs in the wider family along with cancer and coronary defects, although ASF has never been formally diagnosed except in Fran's case. The problem is that we have known about mental illness for over a hundred years, but still do not have a definitive cure, despite medical advances in that time. I also regret not being able to get medical help and advice when we really needed it. Being told by medics to 'keep an eye on her' because they are busy is a bit like saying watch a smoking oil tanker. One day you just know it will all blow up in your face?

My wife and I were trying for a daughter. What God gave us was so much more. Francesca or 'Fran' as she was known to her friends, was slim, beautiful, and dressed down, but no party was ever complete without her. She wasn't really that interested in boys, but loved sports and music, with the Killers and Snow Patrol amongst her favourite bands. She was prolific at swimming, running, and tennis which was her favourite sport. She rarely dressed up for family or formal occasions, but when she did, she could look a million dollars.

This book is intended to complete her legacy to ensure that her life was not in vain or her vast potential wasted. Unfortunately her qualifications she worked so hard for now just sit in a folder. Instead if this book should ever become a movie featuring the positive side of mental health, and her school tennis trophies and archery trophies continue to be awarded in future, then at least something positive will have been achieved.

My Wonderful Fran;

List of Contents.

Chapter 1; Early Days

Fran's story really began where another life ended back in 1990. It was a hot July World Cup final Sunday and we had gone for a walk in the village where we lived when we received an urgent phone call. Colin, my father in law had collapsed whilst on holiday in Cornwall and been rushed to Truro hospital by helicopter from St. Mawes where they had been on holiday with Brenda, his wife. The family had to rush down to Cornwall although some of us, including myself had to stay home and work. Colin was unconscious for several weeks, and was ultimately transferred to Chase Farm Hospital in Enfield by road ambulance which must have been a long and difficult journey, for he did not survive long after.

Colin was a proud professional man, and seeing him in hospital fighting for his life in an unconscious state for almost 2 weeks was soul destroying. I remember him at our wedding, doing the father of the bride's speech with such dry wit and humour. He was a Rotarian and proud of the important work that that organisation did for charity at that time. I also remember him at our house in the summer just before he collapsed, playing with our young boys, James (5) and Adam (4) at that time with such pride. Adam, with his shock of black hair, would be pushing his Matchbox model cars along the top of the patio wall overlooking the garden, whilst James played with his buggy. His loss left a gap in the family which was never filled and left the Harston family seriously diminished both in terms of numbers and standing.

Brenda, his widow was obviously shaken by this, and we helped her through the following months which were tough going, and had to give her moral support. In the meantime my wife and I had been trying for a girl without success, using all manner of recommended strange salt free diets. Then one bank holiday Friday in the August following Colin's passing, I went out for a drink with the boys, including my zany brother Mike who knew how to enjoy himself in style, to try and relax after a busy month. When I came back my wife had drunk a whole bottle of red wine, and insisted we try for a girl that particular night according to her chart, which was successful as she became pregnant soon after.

The months flew past into early 1991, but the UK economy was getting steadily worse with interest rates at 15%, and then I was hit with the bombshell of being made redundant and the whole office closing down in central London, due to a collapse in workload. So for 6 weeks I wrote job application letters galore for surveying posts with little success, whilst sitting in my living room trying to support a young and growing family.

Then the very day that Francesca was due to be born, I had an interview as a loss adjuster, and was offered the position based in Wembley. This was great news, and rushed to tell my wife, Kay, who was in QE2 hospital in Welwyn with her mum Brenda and had broken her waters. This labour was longer than the boys, lasting all day and into the evening, and I remember the midwives had gone for a break shortly before 10pm as there was no sign of progress. Then Francesca's head slowly started to appear around 10.10pm, but with the umbilical cord wrapped around her neck which was a worry, as she could be strangled or damage her mental and physical development. I told Kay to try and not push whilst I rushed for help and fortunately the midwifes came, but Francesca was already half way to being born by then complete with umbilical cord around her neck. She was delivered successfully though and mother and baby were taken home the next day.

Fran's early months were not particularly notable, as I became established in my new job, Kay returned to work part time in a ladies fashion shop with Brenda babysitting, or my mum helping if they were both busy. However we all enjoyed the novelty of having a new baby in the family, as our last child Adam, was born back in 1986, some 5 years previously. She was also the only Granddaughter in our immediate family, and that situation remains the same even now, although I expect we will have grandchildren in the fullness of time, courtesy of my sons, James, and Adam.

Fran loved our sheepdog, Heidi but the only downside was that our sheepdog, Heidi; which we had since 6 weeks old seemed to snarl at her. Having seen reports in the news of young babies and children being savaged by dogs around that time, we were aware that this could be a real risk. So after some agonising discussions with the wider family, and no-one willing to come forward to look after her; we eventually decided to contact the Old English Sheep dog rescue centre which was then based in Lincolnshire. We arranged to drive all the way up there one Sunday in May and said our final goodbyes. This was hard as we had had her for 8 years since we were married and she had been a fabulous pet and part of the family otherwise.

Our family had been decimated somewhat around 1990, losing not only Colin, but my grandmother Emily, Aunt Kit, both of my wife's nans plus Aunt June who could talk and smoke for England. We also lost Alan, Colin's cousin to a heart attack. However other members of the family provided valuable support early in our lives and after Fran's death, especially Brenda, Kay's mum. Francesca though was here for a reason and whatever the reason was, it was probably to provide a role and legacy for both our families that we could relate to in the future. That role meant that she could provide support to my wife as a loving daughter, whilst being her true self with me and realise her ambitions and fulfil her potential despite her all too brief time on this planet.

Not surprisingly our boys James and Adam, who were then about 6 and 4 when Fran arrived, weren't thrilled at losing the limelight to their baby sister. However, they also found that a baby sister was a talking point with other children, who liked to play with her. James wasn't unduly concerned about losing the dog, but Adam was very into animals which was more of a problem, as we didn't decide to have another pet until 2002 for one reason or another, which was some 10 years later.

Fran's early years were notable for being paraded at the Nan's homes at dinner and Fran was often dressed up in the latest outfits. We spent her first Christmas in the Lake District in a house rented from a friend which was freezing I remember. We took many pictures of her dressed up and she looked a million dollars, and she was so happy to have a new Barbie doll for Christmas that she went round showing everyone, which was hilarious.

My job involved taking lots of photos of buildings, so I took plenty of photos of the young Francesca with her brothers and family at the right time. We went on holiday the following may to the Italian Lakes, as Brenda was on her own, and thought it would be nice to spend a week in the sun with her daughter and new grand-daughter. This was 6 months before Claire, her cousin had been born. We spent a nice week in the lakes, although the flight out was very bumpy as we flew right through a violent storm in northern France. We still have a nice photo of Fran as a baby taken on one of the islands in Lake Maggiore.

The next few years were not particularly notable, although Francesca was dressed up in bright red coat whilst the boys went tobogganing down our local road the following winter as we had snow, which was a novelty after a series of wet winters. She was walking freely by this time.

I also filmed Francesca's first visit to 'Play world' at London Colney where she played with the boys and their friends although struggled to keep up, getting bogged down in the ball pit full of brightly coloured plastic balls. She kept us amused with her lovely smile and trying to talk, and we laughed when she described her elder brother as disgusting, but it sounded more like 'gusting.'

She eventually moved from a cot into a child's bed and developed her own wardrobe with my wife's expert knowledge of girls and ladies fashion.

By 1994 she was talking and when we went on holiday to Centreparcs with the family around this time, she was learning to ride a bike with stabilizers, and have photos of her doing this in the spring sunshine at Longleat village.

We had several happy years visiting Centreparcs at Longleat watching our new daughter growing up before our eyes.

We also started taking holidays in Sorrento in Italy as I became more established in my job, and took the boys and Francesca as a toddler in a pushchair to a budget hotel in Sorrento called the 'Aminta' from about 1992 onwards on a number of occasions. She enjoyed the sunshine and warm climate and also started meeting other children of her age which was important for her development.

She was starting to grow into a delightful little girl by this time, dressed in all the latest fashions and traditional little girl's outfits. She even wore a traditional Swiss dress that looked simply fantastic on her. I particularly remember her photographed in a dark blue 'Moschino' girls dress.

On the wider front, we had had our kitchen replaced and things were going well until late 1994. My firm had floated on the London Stock Exchange earlier that year and I had bought my wife a new car with our bonus. We also had more holidays as a result. Unfortunately, like everything it didn't last and by the year end, I was made redundant as the company had to make cutbacks to balance the books.

Fortunately the normal surveying business had started to pick up by then, and I was offered a temporary job with Shell UK before moving onto London Underground's Jubilee Line Project which was a fascinating job but not well paid but did include free rail travel as a perk. I stayed with them for 2 years to 1996 whilst Fran was fast growing into the daughter we always imagined she would become with her own charming and sunny personality and a smile that would light up any room.

Chapter 2; Our Little Angel

As Francesca grew and developed, she had a beautiful smile and disposition which came across wonderfully in her school playgroup photos taken at Prae Wood and later at St. Michael's junior school and Harpenden Prep school. At this stage she was dark haired, although not particularly long, petite at about 4 foot high and slim build, and loved wearing all sorts of clothes Kay would dress her up in. It was certainly great fun to have a little daughter you could dress up as a dolly wearing designer makes of children's clothes, which you couldn't do with her brothers. We have a photograph of Fran, aged about 3 holding a small umbrella and looking absolutely radiant.

James her elder brother was about 5 foot high at this time with fair hair and slim build. Adam, his younger brother a bit smaller at 4 foot six inches with dark hair and a little podgy.

I was six foot 4 inches high and slim build with dark hair which sadly started going white from age 42 onwards with constant job worries. Kay, my wife was about 5 foot 5 inches high and pretty with medium length blonde hair, and a fetish for expensive designer clothes. Brenda, her mum, was a godsend and helped with the family, often visiting with packets of chocolate bars and goodies for the kids which they looked forward too when nanny visited.

Fran was developing nicely into the caring and loving daughter we had always wished for. She showed concern for the welfare of others and was happy to watch whilst the other children played at playgroup or school to see what they were doing.

We also had occasional visits from my brother Mike, who was an occupational therapist and talented grade 8 musician, and was about 6 foot 2 inches high with fair hair and of slim build. He was married to Pam who was shorter with dark hair. My sister Kim who was married to Dan, an American living in the UK; was about 5 foot ten inches high, and had a son called John who was Fran's first cousin dark haired and was about a year older than Fran.

We would spend some weekends at the nannies houses on Sundays, with little Francesca playing in the back garden with her dollies, all dressed up for the occasion with her beautiful smile.

She left Prae Wood Infants School near us to go to St. Michael's junior school where she started to interact with older children which she found more challenging after the age of 5.

My wife suggested she should go to private school instead, although I wasn't keen, so we looked at Harpenden Prep school for a few years, but this later turned out to be a mistake, as she was bullied and came home crying on occasions. She enjoyed going to school, but because she was shy and bashful, she was picked on by older children who could be quite ruthless. There was also a problem here later on that resulted in the school later being closed down and reopening as a Nursery instead.

That resulted in Francesca being moved around the age of 8 and a half to Stormont School in Potters Bar, which was close to her 2 nannies, who could pick her up or drop her off in an emergency or if the roads were bad. Stormont was a genuinely nice reassuring private girl's junior school where initially she took a little time to settle but made new friends and developed into her own little persona.

She later developed into a delightful little girl who loved dancing, swimming, and running and all manner of sports, including skiing as she went to France with the school, and hockey. I remember going to her final day at Stormont with Kay and Brenda, and feeling so proud when she was awarded an illustrated book on dogs which she loved.

She continued going to Centreparcs with the family every year at Longleat around every spring/ summer, and sometimes the boys would go off with my parents to Perth and Gleneagles in Scotland as they liked to play golf, whilst staying at the Hydro centre.

The majority of Fran's friends from Stormont School unfortunately went onto Princess Helena College in Hitchin, which was some way to the North. Fran made many new friends after moving schools but sadly lost touch with many of her original friends and contacts. Francesca found it difficult to make new friends initially as her personality made her shy and reticent. Also being transferred from a small school of several hundred to over 1000 girls was daunting in the extreme for a young 11 year old, with little worldly experience of life.

Whilst at Stormont, Francesca suddenly ran out in the road in front of the school for no reason one day, and was diagnosed as suffering from Asperger's syndrome shortly afterwards, and that's where her real story begins.

Chapter 3; My 42nd Birthday

For my 42nd birthday, we decided to go to Italy for 2 weeks in July with the boys and Francesca, despite this being relatively expensive. We stayed at the Aminta hotel, which was a comfortable family hotel situated on a hill overlooking the town with fantastic views across the bay of Naples and Mediterranean Sea. You could see all the cruise liners in the bay, stopping over at Sorrento below. We would also visit the Hotel President nearby for coffee, whilst the kids would be playing at the kids club or watching videos with their new found friends.

The swimming pool at the Hotel Aminta; I remember was quite deep for children, but they all loved the diving boards and would fool around for hours here with their friends, including Fran who was play acting in front of them. It was here that she learned to swim properly and became a phenomenal swimmer, and could swim for hours.

We also visited the Isle of Capri which was hot and busy with tourists, and took some wonderful pictures of Francesca dressed up in her Swiss and Italian dresses which were a real picture. My wife, Kay and Francesca sat on a park bench in the town with Francesca holding her treasured teddy, Laura, whilst staring at the fantastic view across the Bay of Naples towards the volcanic landscape of Mount Vesuvius. I would envisage Madonna's song *Isaac* as the soundtrack to such a wonderful vista. I particularly remember a photo of her on the park bench outside the *Communale di Sorrento* or town hall at the time, which had neatly manicured grass lawns enclosed by railings. This had pathways in between, and was a favourite haunt of couples after dark going out on the town, as the main street was closed to traffic until midnight at weekends for people to stroll and window shop.

The day of my birthday was memorable, as we had a busy day sight- seeing and shopping in the town until late before getting the bus back to the hotel. It was then that the real drama started. We all sat down for a birthday dinner outside on the terrace with a wonderful view whilst having dinner, with some of the kids' friends joining us also. However the skies over Naples were darkening with a huge storm brewing.

After dinner we joined the party inside the hotel dining room, where the family run hotel baked a huge lemon cake, divided up into 100 pieces, and served to all the holiday guests. We then drank wine and liqueurs and danced to the sounds of the *Maccarena* whilst sitting on the floor doing a rowing boat action. Francesca hugely enjoyed the dancing with me acting as her dance partner as the boys wanted to show off, as they do.

Whilst the dancing continued, flashes of lightning appeared over Naples and the noise grew in the distance. At first the party continued unabated, but as the night wore on the children tired and the storm grew until lightning flashed across the entire bay and hit the top of the Hotel which was high up, knocking out the lights and music out for several minutes until the generator could cut in. The party continued but by this time the storm was raging outside with torrential rain and winds blowing the metal chairs and tables around like ninepins. It was about midnight by then, so we decided to stop for the day and retire in no uncertain terms whilst the worst of the storm abated. Fortunately in foreign countries storms seem to last for a short duration and blow over fairly quickly, unlike in the UK.

My birthday may have only lasted a day but remains long in the memory as being such an unusual and celebratory day, with a combination of circumstances which is unlikely to be matched ever again.

Chapter 4; Fran's final days at Stormont and starts at STAGS.

Fran's final year at Stormont in 2002 was a happy one, despite being diagnosed with ASF the previous year. She worked hard and seemed more focussed, particularly enjoying the swimming galas at Queenswood School on Saturday mornings during the school year.

She threw herself wholeheartedly into her studies and spent time with her nanny, Brenda as kay worked some days and I had to drop her off at school. She was developing into a wonderful little girl aged 11 on 19th April of her final year.

She had made many new friends during this time and went to spend time with them locally, and enjoyed their company. She also went ski-ing to the French Alps in her final year, and took to ski-ing like a duck to water by all accounts, a bit like her dad back in the 1970's who had skied all over much of Europe and in the USA back then.

Kay went to see Fran take part in her sports day, which was pretty much like any other, and she came back with a collection of medals, mainly for swimming which she excelled at after learning to swim in Sorrento on holiday. Kay was so proud to see her little girl doing well in school sports competitions, and growing into a confident little girl with the world at her feet.

With the academic year coming to a climax and her time at Stormont girls school which was private gradually ebbing away, it was a disappointment that many of her friends were going off to Princess Helena College in Hitchin, some way away. Only one friend, also called Francesca, ended up going with her to STAGS the following year and a new secondary all-girls school. However her other friend, Francesca Hawes, lost touch once they started at STAGS and developed new friends as girls of that age tend to do.

Entry to STAGS was by no means a sure thing, as Fran and Kay had to attend interviews with the then headmistress; the diminutive but absolutely wonderful Mrs Murrell who was like everyone's favourite aunt, who later retired in 2010 with several other staff including her music teacher. He was also a wonderful timeless character who retired in 2012 to Devon, and was a great loss to the school. He was last known to be employed part time as a ticket inspector on the North Devon railway, which was one of his hobbies apparently. Entry to secondary school was also dependent upon academic performance and Fran had worked hard to secure her place. She had even attended an interview at Parmiters' school with Kay, which was a mixed school near Watford where both of her brothers, James and Adam had attended; but she chose STAGS over Parmiters, as she felt it was a better learning environment for her in an all-girls school where there would be fewer distractions for her.

Fran's finale at Stormont was quite memorable as Kay and I were summoned to a prize-giving day where all the students work was displayed and parents could wander around the school and thank the teachers for their work. Fran's name was called and she proudly walked up to collect her prize of a book on dogs, which she had specifically asked for in recognition for her effort that year in achieving the best performing student award. She was incredibly pleased with herself and enjoyed the summer after breaking up in early July before going on holiday with her nanny, the wonderful Brenda. She would often take Fran out and they would go out to local places and enjoy tea and traditional cakes and spend quality time bonding together whilst Kay and I were at work.

Back in August 1999 we had moved house, and upon clearing out the garage came across 2 massive spiders, which I sensed was a sign that our lives were going to change for the better ostensibly in future, big time. At the exact moment we left our old house at 12 noon, there was a solar eclipse which was eerie as the sun visibly dimmed and we watched through special glasses as the moon obstructed the sun.

We had exchanged contracts whilst we were on holiday at Perranporth in Cornwall with the boys wearing their Lazio and Milan shirts and Fran wearing her bikini, but she was still very skinny and of a petite build at that time. I specifically remember a photo of her curled up the rocks near the beach being playful with the boys, who spent most of the day doing what boys do best, which is non-stop ball games and annoying everyone they seemed to come into contact with.

Chapter 5; Fran takes up Archery and makes new friends

The summer passed before we knew it and after several years of taking up archery I had shot a blinder that summer, setting a series of club and county records and later going on to win the GNAS gold medal for handicap improvement. When Fran started STAGS, she asked if she could come along and try archery with me one Sunday morning at Sandpit Lane in St. Albans, which is where we shot outdoors during the summer season. After completing her training course, I said yes so she came along in tow one Sunday and introduced her to everyone at the club. It was here that she met important new friends in her life who were not tied to her school, but showed her that sport could open doors into a number of new fields and meet new people.

This was important as she had struggled to make friends with Asperger's Syndrome, and found this a heaven sent opportunity to fill her mobile phone up with a whole load of exciting new contracts. She said she only did it for fun but shot a blinding score of -18 below handicap to win the GNAS gold medal for the year following my win. Fran loved to swim and jog, but her introduction to archery also saw her make some important new friends as it turned out for her life.

This included Chris, and several others, but it was Mary, Lucy, and Katherine who she shot mostly with and formed the basis of the club team for 5 years. In that time, they literally cleaned up with Mary taking a series of awards and the junior girls team enjoying being runners up at county level several times and winning it in 2003. Fran went on to achieve 5 club records and 1 county record, 2 of which were surpassed but 4 still stand today in her honour.

Her friend Mary did extremely well and went on to represent England archery at youth team level before going onto University at Portsmouth later on.

Fran's early days at STAGS academically went very smoothly and without incident, although she made a number of new friends and tended to drift away from her friend from Stormont who had started with her as she was in a different class.

Holidays in the early days at STAGS were with Brenda, her nanny or with us and the rest of the family including grandparents at Centreparcs, Longleat where we went for 3 or 4 years then, and knew the place inside out.

In 2004 we did take her away with Kay and me and left the boys with the grandparents at Perth as they wanted to spend some quality time with the grandchildren. It also allowed Kay and me to bond with Francesca whilst spending 2 weeks in Sorrento Italy, where we took some nice photos. Fran made several new friends whilst there from Essex but the relationship didn't really continue after the holiday which was a bit disappointing. Fran started to become a little podgy and became concerned about her weight for the first time, although she still looked very fit to us, and made Kay look a bit 'mumsy' by comparison.

Fran was developing into a wonderful daughter by this stage and becoming a real asset to my little family of 5. She also supported us wholeheartedly when some other members of the family perhaps did not. A word about Brenda, her grandmother, who spoke excitedly in a high pitched voice and thought the world of Fran, and would bring her chocolates and goodies every time she visited or 'baby-sat' the boys and Fran, although James was in 6th form and 18+ by this time, and occasionally would babysit for the other 2.

In June 2005, Mary, Fran's friend from Archery with Chris and several other boys took Fran to an Archery fun day at Hertford where she had something of a field day. She was a bit reticent at first, but dressed all in blue she won the recurve prize and came second in bare bow and won the Lady Paramount's prize for her favourite Archer on the day, with her friend Mary cleaning up in the compound stakes. Fran also took part the following year, winning the bare bow prize and Mary taking the compound. She later wanted to concentrate on her studies so the archery took a back seat after 2006 including the junior team. Lucy and Katherine who were good friends were a bit older and moved onto university soon afterwards and Fran saw them less often after that.

During this time, Fran showed no signs of her ASF affecting her performance academically or in sport. She also took up tennis, which became her favourite sport of all, although she also tried Badminton with her cousin, and rowing during the summers of 2005/ 6 and also squash every Saturday.

So every Saturday morning for 2 years, Dad would drive Fran to Broxbourne lakes to do rowing at 9am, followed by driving back to St. Albans to do squash about 11.30 and Badminton at 5pm, which was exhausting. Wednesdays were her tennis days and I would have to pick her up from Harpenden about 6pm, as she would get the bus from STAGS about 4pm normally and hated missing tennis for any reason. She said she gave the youngsters she played against a head's start, but she was a formidable player, as confirmed by her brothers and Cousin John, who wasn't bad himself.

As the days and weeks passed, Francesca grew into a delightful little girl and became a teenage girl, which was something of a novelty for us, having had boys and their cousin John also being a boy about a year older.

At school Francesca seemed to breeze through the schoolwork and seemed happy at home by herself and reading and doing sports, usually with friends out of school rather than at school. Her previous Asperger's Syndrome diagnosis at the age of nine did not seem to matter at this age, as she was progressing well with valuable feedback from her teachers and school, who all said she was a delight to teach and responded well. Her only faults were that she loved to talk and would annoy the librarian by making noise in the quiet areas and also was shy. However she also had no fear and a wonderful sense of innocence that is all too rare these days, apart from her wonderful smile for which she became renowned as she could quite literally light up a room like no one else I know, even when you were feeling down.

In 2005, Kay and I went to Switzerland to ride the Glacier Express from St. Moritz to Zermatt, which is something I had always wanted to do, but never previously had the opportunity or the time to do. Fran spent time at home with Brenda babysitting her and the boys, who were older teenagers by this time. Fran loved this as nanny would bring round bag loads of chocolates, and her friends would all tuck into this chocolate bonanza about once a week.

Occasionally I would look at Fran and she seemed odd, or in a different world. This was so when the family took photos of her at my mum and dad's place during family events or in her room when her female friends used to came round and take photos, usually with their latest camera phones at that time. Smartphones were not common place at that time so, Fran had a clam shell type phone, which still remains in her room, fully charged and is still fully workable. However we thought nothing of it at that time, but you could see a glazed expression from time to time. However to her credit, she pressed on with life and would enjoy archery with her friends at weekends, plus swimming and others sports such as badminton with cousin Claire at Bricket Wood sports centre, before it closed; or squash on Saturdays at what used to be called Cannons Highfield (now Nuffield Health) in St. Albans, UK where we lived.

Chapter 6; Fran's mid-teenage years; the Maid in the Mist.

By 2005, things were going fairly well overall for Francesca and our family as a whole. Fran had become established at school and was progressing well, and had an established circle of regular friends she would see, This involved Dad driving her to see friends all over the locality at all hours of the day and night, as parents tend to do.

Workwise we had been doing well with Kay moved to Bolton's ladies fashion from her previous job, with me earning record figures as the housing market had picked up and boomed, which increased demand for our services with KFH at the time. Fran took an interest in my work and actually came into my office for a day once a year as part of her course, with what was known as' take your daughter to work day.' I showed her round whilst I had to do a flat survey in Hampstead before returning to my office which was based in Bayswater around 2003. She later came into Harrow which is where I now work out of as a consultant these days, supposedly semi-retired although still working hard it seems.

By 2006 we had had a bumper year the previous year, and discussed the idea of taking Kay and Fran to Canada for a transcontinental trip lasting 3 weeks.

It may be a rare chance to see the world, and we wanted to share it with our daughter as the boys were already grown up and going away on their own holidays by this time, with girlfriends. James was 22 and at University by this time, and I was taking his stuff up and down to Warwick at the beginning and end of every term, and sorting out his lodgings, as he was in rented housing by the 2nd and final years of his law degree.

So, we faced the situation and booked to go on an escorted tour of Canada for 3 weeks for the three of us. We decided to go Red Leaf as Gold leaf was more expensive for 3 than 2, as Fran counted as an adult at 15. So we flew out of Heathrow on the long flight to Toronto our first stop and arrived late afternoon. We watched the news and were surprised that all flights had been cancelled due to a terrorist threat just after we left so were lucky, but also effectively were stranded out there.

The hotel and Toronto were just great, as were in a Multi storey hotel with rooftop pool, and views across the city and great lake. As soon as we arrived, Fran decide to go for a jog after the long flight but didn't tell us where she was going, so we panicked and spent ages looking for her. Apparently we later found out that she had jogged around the block, but as it turned out, Toronto is one of the safest cities in the world and one of the most pleasant; despite its harsh cold winters, so the shopping malls are below ground rather than at street level. The weather was fantastic when we arrived, basking in 27 degrees of sun, and taking drinks in a bar overlooking the lakeside. We spent several days in this wonderful city and Fran really enjoyed the breakfast syrup pancakes!

Whilst in Toronto, we visited the world famous CN tower, although I was stopped at security in the light of the recent terrorist threat, as they were taking no chances. However we were eventually allowed through and looked around the glass floor at the top of the tower and took pictures all around Toronto with some breath taking views as it was a bright clear day, so you could see for miles literally. We could see the plains to the north and Hudson Bay, and across the lake and city below. Fran meanwhile was busy dancing on the glass floor looking down to see a bus the size of a sugar cube below and took photos galore whilst dancing. The observation level was filled with numerous excited tourists, mostly Japanese and Chinese children on holiday at this time of year, so getting space to see the marvellous views was a bit of a challenge.

After the CN tower we went for lunch at a hotel near Niagara, which we all loved, before going on to see the falls themselves at close quarters. Fran being the adventurer in our party decided to go off with some of our tour group and join the 'Maid in the Mist.' Decked out in blue waterproofs and boots, she boarded the ship and they disappeared into the mist at the foot of the Horseshoe Falls which were thunderous. She returned wet and with a new addition - a 'Maid in the Mist' peaked cap she had taken a liking to. We spent some time admiring the falls and sheer amount of water pouring over the waterfall, before returning to our coach and guide. We had to wait as some of our party had decided to take a helicopter ride over the falls, but reported they felt sick afterwards, so don't regret giving that a miss.

Following that we proceeded on to a little village called Niagara on the Lake nearby where we spent a magical afternoon. The village was like a period film set with mid-western US houses painted white with balconies, and the tiniest church I have ever seen. The area was largely traffic free and even boasted a preserved bright red no.8 London Bus in pristine condition on display for tourists. This made us all feel right at home.

It was here that we decided to take afternoon tea outside a little period cafe, and Fran indulged in her favourite past time of seeing if she could get Pistacchio ice cream, and French raspberry-ade which was her favourite drink.

All in all it was an exhausting but memorable day and we returned to our hotel in down town Toronto to enjoy a late evening meal and swim in the indoor rooftop pool. We then watched some Canadian TV before retiring, as the following day we had to fly out west to continue the rest of our Canadian adventure.

Chapter 7; Fran discovers the Rockies and her alter ego.

We were up early the following day and packing ready for the coach to go to the airport. Our tour guide assembled everyone after a last syrup pancake breakfast which Fran savoured before jogging round the block of skyscrapers before joining our party.

The transfer was fairly short and I remember waiting in the lounge for some time. It was here we saw the media reports about a terrorist threat at Heathrow and suspending all flights just after we had left UK airspace.

We checked in whilst Fran was busy listening to her iPod and latest Snow Patrol album, *Eyes Open*, which had just been released that month. We checked in and the security guard took exception to Fran's manicure kit which included scissors, which he confiscated much to our surprise. It seems that they were taking no chances after the recent events at Heathrow.

We eventually went to the terminal gate overlooking the tarmac at Toronto before boarding a smaller Air Canada plane for Calgary, than the one we arrived on. The flight was fairly uneventful; flying over the prairies, forest, and lakes, and we only had drinks and snacks surprisingly, so were quite hungry when we arrived. The terminal at Calgary was odd, as we seemed to disembark into a shopping area with a large dinosaur I remember which Fran found very amusing.

We then were taken by coach out of Calgary towards Banff in the Rockies. The drop in temperature was noticeable - from a sunny 26 degrees in Toronto to just 8 degrees and cloudy in Banff, following showers in mid-August. We checked into our hotel and Fran took a picture of Kay and me in the street looking towards the Rockies I recall.

Unfortunately we could only afford the 'red leaf' hotel at the time, which was a basic hotel in the high street, straddled with pick-up trucks and American cars. By this time we had gone from t-shirts and shorts to thick woolly jumpers. We went along to see what the gold leaf package had to offer, and had tea at the Fairmont, Banff. This resembled a baronial Scottish castle overlooking a championship level golf course below the foothills of the Rockies. I was amused to see the railway station was a simple affair, with a train every 2-3 days or so, depending on the season.

We also took the opportunity to play tennis here with Kay and Fran donning borrowed rackets to play her favourite game. During the course of the match, we were astounded to see a large deer or mousse walk past the court on the south side, and munch a mouthful of tree leaves.

The courtier at the Fairmont warned us that the area was full of wildlife with tales of black bears and coyotes frequenting the golf course early and late in the day, although Grizzly bears were rarely seen round here.

Our stay in Banff was all too brief, but it reminded us of Scotland very much. Indeed many of the railroad pioneers of the Canadian National and Canadian Pacific days were captured in photos on the walls of many of the public buildings in the town, and hotels. The river passing through the town was very wide and we realised that we were heading towards the wilderness.

Next stop was Lake Louise, where the gold leaf members of our escorted party were staying at the Fairmont here. This was a traditional hotel overlooking the lake and mountain in the background, but I found it nice but nothing special. What surprised Fran was the bear proof bins, and tales of the local bakery shop at Lake Louise village being invaded by black bears on occasions.

We then proceed up to Moraine Lake, which was a fabulous location for tourists. Kay stayed at the bottom of the mountain, but Fran and I climbed up the path to the top, and asked a Japanese tourist to take a picture of the two of us. I also took a picture of Fran at the top and landscape scenes, but that picture of the two of us has turned out to be the most iconic photo of Fran and I which is on my phone, computer and just about everything else. It had a timeless, almost telepathic quality which is rare. Colin Mold's 'Prayer and Shelter' would be the soundtrack to this iconic setting, with Fran spinning with her outstretched arms in the air, savouring the moment and sheer joy of being at peace with herself.

The 'Red Leaf' party continued up a long road towards Emerald Lake, where we were due to stay. The coach turned off the road up a long drive and towards a small settlement of houses around Emerald Lake. Fran's eyes bulged as we saw a bright green lake mirroring the conifer forest with traditional timber houses with log fires set in the forest. This was a truly stunning location, used by Marilyn Monroe by all account in the past for privacy after one of her celebrated marriages.

We went for a walk and saw several people taking a dip in the lake, but they said it was cold despite being a sunny afternoon. We unpacked and walked around the village location and lakes, admiring the scenery, and taking some wonderful photos of the landscapes. We were warned however by the guide that a young woman had been killed whilst out jogging by the side of the lake unescorted one morning recently, so we were advised to stay close to the village.

That evening we assembled at the main restaurant in the village and our guide was reminiscing about other tours he had led to Canada and elsewhere. Some of the party took the opportunity of using one of the hot tubs, and during the evening you could hear the calls of wolves and coyotes in the distance, as we were now right in the Canadian wilderness. Emerald lake was a magical place, but made me feel nervous with all the howling during the night. The following morning, Fran and Kay posed for pictures, with Fran holding a shopping bag and hat in front of the lake before we set off for Jasper.

The journey to Jasper seemed to take forever, and we stopped for sandwiches at a picnic stop on our journey through the Rockies, noting the Crow's Foot glacier and another glacial bright green lake in the everlasting temperate forest.

Eventually we came to the Columbian Ice field, where some of our party elected to go on the ice buses. Fran, Kay, and I elected to stay at the visitor centre and do some window shopping and have a break instead for an hour or so.

We continued our journey until we pulled into Jasper and our motel for several nights. We arrived in the midst of a summer storm, with a beautiful rainbow to the east of the town. We walked around and Fran enjoyed a specialist sweetshop she found in the town, with all sorts of candy bars and chocolate animals. After dinner, we watched a bit of TV to play catch up on world news, as we had been 'out of range' of civilisation for 2-3 days, before retiring. We also had mobile phone reception again which was a novelty.

The following morning I awoke early whilst Kay and Fran were still sleeping, about 5 am when it was still dark. I glanced out of the window but was amazed to see Coyotes wandering the streets, searching for cats and small animals to eat. Bears also come into the town occasionally, but are a problem at the railroad yard we were told. It seems they like the maize cars, especially when wet and the maize ferments, making a sort of brew that bears find Moorish and leaves them rolling around half drunk. I woke Fran and showed her the Coyote at the crossroads opposite, and she said, 'oh yeah.'

That day, Kay decided to stay in town and read a novel, whilst Fran and I went white water rafting on the Athabasca River. This was a wide river from the town, and we were driven several miles out of town to board a large inflatable raft with about 30 people, wearing life jackets. Fran sat at the head of the raft to catch as many waves as possible, and got chatting to some American girls whom she exchanged experiences with. At first the river was quite benign, but we went round some bends in to whirlpools and were soon tossed around with plenty of splashes, although not too badly as we had a large raft. It was a fine sunny day by this time and the temperature had risen from Banff to a warmer 15 degrees or so in the sun, although cool in the evenings. We posed for a picture taken from a nearby bridge over the river, which we still have.

We packed up and the following day, we left Jasper by train early in the morning. It was misty that day and we had breakfast whilst passing through the wilds of Alberta. At first the scenery was lakes and forest, giving way to prairies and farmland and some towns. We stopped at Prince Regent for an hour or so for lunch, and allowed long freight trains to pass on long passing loops on this route. We went via the northern route, although would have preferred the southern route via Kamloops and the Fraser river, which has better scenery. However on this route we saw plenty of bears, some sitting on the track chewing maize, as it was warm there.

Evening came and we arrived at a strange place called Quesnel. This was like an old peoples home where the average age was over 70. The hotel was strange and the town eerily quiet. Kay couldn't wait to leave, but Fran and I wandered down to the river bank and spent some quality father daughter time together watching the otters play in the wide, fast flowing river.

We left Quesnel early the following day and proceeded toward Whistler. The scenery changed on the second day, to a drier, dusty landscape following the twisting river between the hills. The weather was sunny and warmed as we closed on Whistler. We rounded a lake before coming across the valley to a river bridge, where we stopped by a Red Indian settlement, sadly now all in stainless Winnebago's but still fishing using traditional methods.

Whistler was a million miles from Quesnel in every way. It was young, dynamic, and bustling with modern buildings and geared to sport, with the upcoming winter Olympics due to be held there and in Vancouver.

We checked in at our hotel, which was clean and modern, before taking a wildlife tour to check out bear habitats. Kay and I went on this one, whilst Fran decided to chill out and listen to music in the hotel. We saw a bear hole under a tree where they hibernate and also a rubbish tip where just after 5pm, when all then operatives left for the day; wildlife appeared almost by magic, with a coyote walking right in front of our position, a bear with 2 cubs breaking cover and other smaller animals and birds flocking, including a sea eagle.

We had a great meal out that evening in the town square but found Whistler a bit pricey. The following day, we all went up the chairlift to the top of Mount Whistler, where Fran walked around and we took some photos, before returning. Fran tried out her phone video here I remember.

We then said farewell to Whistler before heading out for Vancouver. We noted the skunks at one of the parks, before going up to the nature reserve by cable car, which was really busy with tourists and kids. Fran and I also went across the long and wobbly suspension bridge to the island reserve, and received a certificate, although Kay didn't manage it. On the way back, we stopped for some time to admire two 6-year old Grizzly bear cubs which were being cared for on the mountain. Fran laughed as they scratched each other's backs and lounged around in the water on what was becoming a hot day.

We arrived at our hotel which was a multi storey point block, with an open balcony, and Fran went out and we told her to come in but she refused. We were worried about her safety but she relented eventually.

There was also a basement pool where Fran and I went for a swim that evening. We walked around the city, but most of our party decided to go off to Vancouver Island, which was delayed in the heat by all accounts. I had a row with Kay that day, after Fran had snatched a 20 dollar bill and given it to a street beggar. However, we made up and went off to see

Stanley Park and the totem poles, and the Aquarium which was a memorable day. The tanks of fish and so on were great, but it was the old otter sunbathing and the display by the ghostly Beluga whales that sticks in the memory. Fran also posed with a large tawny Owl for a great picture.

We returned to the hotel for one last meal, before saying farewell to Vancouver, the Pacific Ocean and Canada and a wonderful holiday and going to the airport for the long flight home, which was very busy that night. We tried to sleep but Fran stayed awake all night on the flight, excited by listening to the latest Snow Patrol album, *Eyes Open.*

Chapter 8; Exam year at school and coming to terms with her condition.

After Canada, things went fairly quiet for a while, with nothing out of the ordinary happening for some months. She also seemed much happier in herself, having been on a major trip abroad had given her a new perspective on things. On the archery front, Fran had scaled back her exploits whilst still keeping in touch with her many friends at this time. She continued with her early morning paper round before school to continue earning some pocket money mainly spent on sweets, drinks, and music like most teenagers.

Fran returned to school facing mock exams in January 2007, so she was pre-occupied in doing well in preparation for those.

Fran continued with her breakneck schedule or playing badminton Saturdays or Sundays with her cousin, and also swimming weekday evening and do rowing Saturday mornings at Broxbourne before rushing back to play squash with other juniors at Cannons leisure centre, St. Albans. However this exhausting schedule took its toll, and she gradually cut back on some of her non-stop sports schedule which was slowly wearing out mum and dad with fatigue.

Fran continued to be a delightful girl in the autumn of 2006, and music continued to be a big part of her life. Her interest in Snow Patrol and the Killers was undiminished, but she also took an interest in the Editors and even some of her dad's U2 CDs, often played in the car on the way to various sporting venues.

Fran continued to see her many friends at this time, although juggling exam studies and friends was tricky - so she simply invited them round to help with revision on occasions. However in late summer this would result in trips to the sweet shop and playful antics in the park during the warm late summer evenings, to the tune of TATU and 'All the things she said' whilst running without a care in the world.

Fran continued to do archery although when we went indoors for the winter at STAGS in October, Fran and her 3 archery friends; Katherine, Mary and Lucy spent an entire session talking, much to the chagrin of the field judge that day, the rotund and distinctive James Rose. He politely reminded them that they were there to shoot, not talk for England.

Life continued fairly uneventfully through the autumn. So much so that Paul and Kay managed to take a short break in Geneva whilst Brenda looked after the boys and Fran at home to give them a break. James, Adam, and Fran enjoyed Brenda's presence as she would bring round handfuls of chocolates and goodies, and of course like to cook a full English breakfast, as mum and dad usually preferred continental, which the kids did not.

Fran would often ride in the passenger seat of Dad's car which was a 2006 registered Saab saloon at this time, which was retained until 2008 when it was changed for a Mazda 6 estate. She would also sit in the passenger seat of Kay's car, which was a 2006 registered small Audi TT convertible, although we hardly ever had the top down due to uncertain British summer weather.

Dad would ferry Fran to and from school most days, although occasionally she would walk the 2 miles or so to school or get a lift with a friend's mum. Sometimes this meant Dad having to change his schedule to accommodate Fran; although Dad was still working full time for KFH at this time, but the economic slowdown was becoming apparent with fewer instructions and daily jobs. Little did we know how hard things would get over the coming 5 years or so?

The autumn of 2006 was unremarkable, and Fran continued to work hard at school on her GCSEs, with her mock exams in January of 2007, just after Christmas. She was predicted reasonable grades for each subject and by and large achieved these in the January mocks. However Kay and I were worried that she was coming under increasing pressure at school and how that might affect her condition. If it did, she hid it remarkably well for there were no outward signs of stress or unusual behaviour at this time.

I remember Fran was also continuing with Guides every Monday night in St. Albans and would take her there so she could join in activities with her new circle of friends. She seemed to have circles of friends in each area, such as school, archery, guides, and sport, respectively.

It was about this time that Fran had run away and kept talking about 'getting across water' to visit relatives in Ireland, due to voices in her head, although she did not know where they lived. The doctor recommended some routine tests for Fran and recommended she see a Psychologist. A meeting was held at a clinic in central St. Albans after school one day which proved important. Kay and I attended, and the 2 psychologists carried out a report and review of her pastoral care. To our surprise they recommended that she be out on a course of pills to suppress her Asperger's and complications, although it wasn't causing her undue problems at that time, despite a fairly heavy programme of coursework and revision for her summer exams.

This was met with consternation and alarm by Kay and I, and Fran herself as one of the side effects was that this could suppress her memory functions making her lethargic and affecting her academic performance. This was not what we wanted to hear, and Fran herself refused point blank to take any drugs at all, although this is a common trait of people suffering from mental health complaints and ASF.

So Fran decided to continue to study without taking any drugs and we were advised to 'keep an eye' on her during her exams to ensure she wasn't getting stressed out. Fran also went to see her GP at the Lodge surgery once a week for follow up visits, and he suggested that she go to 'Youth Talk,' an organisation locally catering for young people under pressure or suffering from mental health problems, although she never actually attended, we later found out.

One of the big problems we came across was that as Fran was 16, she had privacy rights regarding her own medical affairs, so that our GP would not disclose any of what was discussed between her and her GP, which was frustrating for us as parents, as we did not what issues were discussed or things to look out for? She mentioned voices in her head and also was showering with her swimming costume on as she was worried that people may be watching her. This was after she watched the 'Truman Show,' a film about life being depicted as a large film set, with herself as one of the actors or actresses.

Fran did attend meetings with her GP during the spring of 2007, although we do not know what was discussed or the outcome of those meetings. However she continued studying without taking a course of drugs and seemed unfazed by all the fuss.

Fran decided to continue studying for her GCSE final exams in the summer of 2007 and completed her exams without any distress or incident at that time, which was a relief to us as parents.

She celebrated successfully completing her exams by having a series of days out with friends before going away with mum and dad to Switzerland in August of 2007.

As part of her celebrations, Francesca had booked tickets to see Feeder at Redbourn, which is the county ground about five miles north of St. Albans extremely near to junction nine of the M1 motorway. The ground is used for the county show every May bank holiday and outdoor shows, such as Gymkhana and trade vehicle shows, etc. Fran had booked to go in late August on a hot sultry summer's day without a cloud in the sky.

I picked up her friends from St. Albans before joining a queue of traffic headed for the event, although it wasn't that big in concert terms. Feeder were also playing the northern festival at Loch Lomond the same week as part of a 2 part summer festival with support bands, although the Redbourn one was just Feeder on their own with a brief support act.

I dropped the girls off, as there were about 4 of them, and they went off to buy sweets and souvenirs at sunset, whilst I returned home to watch TV. The evening passed quickly and I later had 3 short phone videos copied to me of the show, which had bright lights and excerpts of feeder tracks, including 'Buck Rodgers' and 'Comfort in Sound'; the lyrics of which suited Fran perfectly in retrospect. The show was a blaze of light and sound from the excerpts I saw, but Fran and her friends said they had a great time, dancing to some favourite singles out around that time.

I later picked the girls up and took them home, as Fran by this time was exhausted as it was dark and getting late around 10.30pm I recall. However it was a clear starry night with a moon and that great feeling you get during the summer concert season of having achieved something worthwhile.

Chapter 9; Switzerland-July 2007

Fran, Kay, and I packed excitedly for our main summer holiday in 2007, which was 2 weeks doing a rail tour across Switzerland. We got dropped off at Luton for check in and ready for our early morning flight to Zurich. Everything went as normal and we departed on time and arrived in Zurich about an hour later but around 9.30 local time. De-planing was swift and efficient at Zurich airport and we boarded the train for the short journey to Zurich *Hauptbahnhof*. Unfortunately we had a run in with the conductor who said we were in first class, although couldn't sit down as the train was busy. He charged us extra for first class despite not being on train more than 10 minutes. Fran thought he was being over-officious.

We detrained and had about an hour to look round Zurich and have a coffee before boarding a wonderful double decker train to Berne on the mainline. This was less busy than the airport train, and gave wonderful views across the plains of northern Switzerland and Bavaria, whilst Fran, Kay and I enjoyed a snack.

We alighted at Berne and had a brief look around this extremely attractive medieval city and capital of the country, including a walk across the high-level river bridge although Fran was not fazed by heights at all.

We took some photos then boarded our next train onto our final destination of Interlaken Ost.

The train wound its way around the edge of the lake, stopping at all stations, including central Interlaken, before terminating about an hour later. It was now early afternoon, so we gathered our bags and made our way the short distance to our period hotel nearby and unpacked ready for dinner that evening.

Dinner was served in the ground floor dining room, and being Switzerland, the menu had a charming picture of a narrow gauge tramcar that plied the nearby Jungfrau mountain range. We were treated to traditional Swiss and Austrian cuisine including Gesuppen and Wienerschnitzel.

We spent a few days exploring Interlaken, and decided to take the narrow gauge mountain train up to the Jungfrau. Fran and Kay posed in the train at Interlaken Ost for a marvellous picture of them both, one of the best photos of the two of them.

The train made its way up to the base of the mountain, where we changed for a cable car. This swung its way up the side of the mountain, with goats and sheep grazing precariously below on the cliff edges. We then changed onto a little tramcar taking us the final leg into the Jungfrau and Murren. This was small traditional Swiss village. There was the option to go on to the observatory overlooking the Aletsch Glacier, but we contented ourselves with a wander around the village. Even in August there was snow on the nearby mountains not far away and it was decidedly cool with clouds hovering over the peaks in shade. The weather that summer unfortunately wasn't good with frequent showers at high and low levels, as the Jetstream was further south than normal, near the northern Mediterranean.

We took some more photos before deciding to return as the clouds were building up ominously. We returned just in time as it absolutely poured with rain the rest of that day.

The following day Fran enquired about going paragliding, as it was something she always wanted to do. At first the paragliding people weren't too keen. We then visited UP paragliding and a young instructor, little more than Fran's age who took a shine to her. He said no problem as long as she was insured, and he would take her up personally and train her in the health and safety procedures before their half hour flight.

So we paid for her to go on a flight plus insurance, and Fran donned her UP helmet and went up to the take-off field at high level. They then went through the pre-flight training routine, whilst Kay and I went down to the landing field in central Interlaken and waited for them.

After a short while, we saw Fran and her instructor run off the cliff edge and glide into the cloudy skies, which was unfortunate as it was sunny to the south over the Jungfrau.

They circled for some time and took a number of pictures of Fran circling about 1000 feet above the town. You could make out the river, railway station and town centre in the photos they took, and which provided timeless memories later.

Gradually they waited their turn as a number of paragliders were coming into land around lunchtime, and saw Fran and her instructor make a perfect landing, before having a group mini-photo-shoot to commemorate a memorable day for Fran.

We spent the rest of the day packing and collecting some souvenirs as we had to leave for Lucerne early the following day.

The train was ready about 9am as we boarded the narrow gauge train at Interlaken Ost for the cross Alps journey to Lucerne. As we said goodbye to Interlaken, which Kay loved, the train made its way into the green undulating hills and countryside before climbing into the hills. The journey became slower as we traversed uneven terrain and stopped at a station at high level with wonderful views each way into the next valley.

Then began the long descent into Lucerne which seemed to take ages, as we seemed to stop everywhere. The weather unfortunately was not abating as it rained frequently with heavy showers in-between. The train eventually wound its way into central Lucerne and we alighted to look for our hotel about half a mile to the south. The hotel was a contrast to Interlaken which was period chalet style Swiss hotel. Lucerne was post- modern international style by contrast. We unpacked and took the tourist train around the city, before walking up the city walls to see the views over the city and lake. We also walked down by the famous bridge and took several memorable photos of Fran and Kay, before walking up to then lion sculpture and fountain, built into a wall.

The showers continued but we had dinner that evening and checked our arrangements for onward travel as we had to head south the following day towards Locarno. This was an unusual journey and I was wrongly charged for first class, which was later refunded as we had pre-booked. Our departure from Lucerne was swift and by paddle steamer from the pier near the station, heading out across the lake. This journey took all day as we passed sailboarders, and stopped on the west side of the lake where an outdoor wedding reception was in progress overlooking the lake. The day was becoming quite sunny and much warmer and more pleasant by this time. We also passed a famous hotel on the east side of the *Vierwaldwattersee* Lake before heading to the pier at Fluelen to connect with the Lotschberg express. Fran and kay had an argument over our 1 course meal, as Fran accused Kay of being selfish but she very rarely had a tantrum like that!

The express pulled in late afternoon at Fluelen and we boarded the first class observation coach. It's not often we travelled first class, but Fran, kay and I could spread out as the coach was almost empty. The train pulled away down the Lotschberg pass and into numerous winding tunnels to drop down to the lower level of Andermatt and interchange with the Glacier Express that Kay and I travelled on back in 2004 without Fran.

The train continued its downward trend following the auto-route heading towards Italy on tall concrete viaduct towering above the railway, river, and plains. We then pulled into a station where travellers for Lugano departed down a separate route, whilst we continued to the end of the line at Locarno.

We then alighted and made our way to the small hotel at the western end of the town square. We arrived in concert season as the town square was closed to traffic, and had tourists milling about and sound system and staging being erected and tested for that Saturday evening's concert.

We checked into our modest accommodation with views across the town square and watched a little TV as Phil Collins was playing Live Aid in Germany with parallel concerts across the globe around that time. Phil Collins being Brenda's favourite artist and always reminds me of her when he plays on the radio.

We had dinner which was a simple affair, but noticed the temperature had risen markedly as it was quite warm. After dinner we had dessert and coffees and sat outside on the terrace to watch the concert that was just starting up with crowds of people gathering in the main square. That evening it was Peter Gabriel playing, and did some new numbers. Eventually he did an encore of his old hits which went down well, despite the thunderstorm over the lake which drenched most concertgoers, with lightning flashes in the hills above.

The following day was Sunday, so Fran and I had some quality 'dad and daughter' bonding time which was all too rare, by taking a paddle boat out on the lake for a heart to heart chat about all the things that are important to girls; exams, boys, money, job, career, hobbies, staying out really late and lifts. We paddled past the disco boat which was being cleared up from the previous evening, with glasses, balloons, and litter everywhere. We enjoyed an hour in the bay before returning and getting ready to depart Locarno for our next destination - Domodossola in northern Italy.

This involved going into the basement of the station at Locarno to board a 2 car electric tram. This made its way out of Locarno and wound up the hills towards the Italian border. Here there was a large semi-circular Steel bridge over a gorge, where we stopped for a brief border check. We then went downhill into a huge valley surrounded by picturesque snow-capped peaks with the town right in the middle. The tram pulled into the terminus underground, so we had to walk up to the main station at ground level.

There we waited for the train to pull in heading back into Switzerland, for Brig and Montreaux. This train was a disappointment as it was an old and battered Italian locomotive hauled train which had seen better days, unlike most of the Swiss trains we travelled on. Eventually we pulled into Montreaux back in Switzerland, but also returned to the Jetstream and wet cloudy weather, leaving the warm sunny weather in Italy and southern Switzerland behind.

The hotel in Montreaux though was one of the best we have ever stayed in. It was the 5 star Grand Hotel and we had asked for an extra night which was worth it. We walked in to the sight of a jazz legend being photographed on the stair for the annual jazz festival which was imminent.

Our room was a large room with TV, film, and bar facilities, and we could also use the spa over the road, which was connected to the hotel by a corridor under the road with views across Lake Geneva or *Lac Leman.*

Fran and Kay wasted no time in changing and going down to use the spa and swimming pool, etc. We also watched a film in our room and later went down to have lunch in the brasserie and dinner in the restaurant.

That evening Fran and I wandered around the jazz festival on the lakeshore as we were both interested in music but Kay was not, and there was a bewildering array of acts. There was everything from well-known artists to new artists and novelty acts performing in makeshift tents. One act was performing on a stage in the lake itself! One German rock act was performing in the street with a bemused small crowd gathering. We also visited the statue of Freddie Mercury, music legend of course who lived in Montreaux before his death.

Kay decided to spend a whole day in the spa, so Fran and I wanted to visit the chocolate factory at Broc. A day she later said was the best of her life as she could indulge herself completely. This involved getting the local mountain train up to a little village in the hills above Montreaux. The station was quaint with books on the platform for passengers to read, and tracks going across the main street with barriers. Here we changed for Gruyere on another local train before getting a tram one stop into the factory at Broc. The weather by this time was cool and wet, but Fran didn't care. She was realising her dream, as depicted in Charlie and the Chocolate factory.

We entered the factory which was free, with few tourists due to the poor weather. We then sat and listened to the history of the factory and chocolate making in French. Fran then walked with me around factory looking at machinery and illuminated diagrams, and particularly the huge array of chocolate samples which made her eyes bulge. We then finished our brief tour lasting an hour with a trip to the shop and she purchased a number of subsidised huge chocolate bars in a large bag.

I then took a photo of her looking very happy on the train on the way back, where the conductor was getting irritated by students wasting time, and delaying the train. The train back was the Glacier Panorama train with large windows to see the passing mountains and scenery.

Sadly our trip to Switzerland and Italy had come to a conclusion, and all that remained was to return to the hotel and pack for the journey home and to be reunited with her brothers, nanny, and our wonderful sheepdog, Topaz.

Chapter 10; 2007-The year the real problems began.

Before returning to school in September 2007, Fran had bought several tickets through me to go to see Feeder, a Welsh rock group who were playing at the county showground at Redbourn in late August. Fran had invited some of her school friends to come with her, and they duly obliged.

It was a hot sultry day, with the concert not due to start until late afternoon with a support act. So dad duly obliged by picking up Mary, one of Fran's friends, although she didn't come onto the concert. I remember driving around Redbourn looking for the youth group at the village hall, which then was an old prefab building which has since been replaced with a modern brick building. We drove around in my then new Mazda 6 grey estate car playing Feeder tracks which Fran and Mary were enjoying, but gave up trying to find the youth group which there was no sign of.

Fran then went to collect her friend, Rabina, later on and one other who met us at the venue. It wasn't that busy surprisingly, as I pulled in to drop Fran off with her fairly new clam style mobile phone, which was all the rage in those days.

I waved them off and said we would pick them up when the gig finished which was about 10.30pm.

Fran used her phone to record some short videos which were a glare of floodlights and noise, so it was difficult to discern what was said and make out the particular Feeder tracks.

However the girls agreed the concert was great fun as they danced to the tracks. The concert was one of two that summer at both Redbourn and Loch Lomond as part of a summer promotion, with Feeder playing both venues, and other groups filling in, although I can't remember all the acts. However I suspect Big Country or Biffy Clyro may have featured somewhere along the line.

After the gig Fran seemed fine, but shortly after restarting school again after the long summer break and holidays she began acting oddly and going on about having to 'cross water.' Kay and I were not sure what this meant so discussed this with councillors and they suggested she should talk to her doctor and Youth talk, but Fran steadfastly refused to attend Youth Talk and would not take drugs.

We had an appointment with 2 NHS Psychiatrists in St. Albans who suggested she take drugs to control her condition, but this ran the risk of affecting her academic performance and to Fran this was simply not negotiable or a realistic option. Fran to be fair did go and talk to her GP about this, but our GP would simply not divulge what was discussed which was very frustrating for Kay and I. She was now 16, and deemed to be independent in terms of medical records, even though she still lived with us as part of our family. This was data protection and bureaucracy being used against us which found infuriating at times. We tried to discuss this direct with Fran but of course she wouldn't discuss what was said with our GP, for fear of it compromising her studies which she regarded as paramount as she still saw herself as having an academic career.

With all this pressure building, and Fran trying to conceal her condition which was starting to become unpredictable, she discussed the idea of going to see her Irish relatives, although she had no details or addresses. Then one day after school, she said she was going out for something and just disappeared, which was every parent's worst nightmare.

The next thing we knew was a phone call from a kindly gentleman at Chester station, saying that our daughter was on a train to Holyhead and should he ask her to return home. It seems he had got talking to Fran as she was travelling alone, and asked where she was going. She said she was going to visit relatives in Irelands, but he said she had no details or ferry ticket, passport, etc. Eventually, to cut a long story short, he spoke to the British Transport police who agreed to take Fran off the train at Chester and said she should return home.

They put her on a train to Wolverhampton, via Wrexham and Shrewsbury as she had to change and wait for a connection. We told her to wait for us, and we would drive up and meet her at Wolverhampton rail station. Obviously this was at the end of a busy working day, so Kay and I were tired but had to get in the car and go and do a further long drive for several hours. We arrived at Wolverhampton by late evening, around 11pm and had to wait until just before midnight when Fran's connecting train pulled in and Fran jumped off the train as if nothing had happened. Kay and I were just relieved to see her safe, as anything could have happened that day. We drove home tired but relieved, and arrived early morning. We decided it was best to have a rest the following day, so cancelled work appointments and Fran took the day off to recuperate.

We then thought everything was fine for a while, although Fran started going on about having to 'cross water' although we said there were no large rivers near us. We found she was starting to become obsessive about this, and one Saturday morning she took off and decided to ride her bright orange Apollo bike down the M1 motorway towards the Thames ostensibly. Needless to say she was spotted by a passing police patrol who arrested her and took her to a carvery at Aldenham near junction 5 of the M1. I then received a call from them asking if I would like to pick up my daughter as she had broken motorway regulations and would have to be picked up as she couldn't ride back on that route. Other roads in the area were busy so I drove down to meet the police motorway patrol who explained the situation and advised me to put the bike in the back of my estate car, which just fitted. We then went home and I told Fran not to do that again as it was dangerous but also embarrassing to pick her up after 2 such incidents in close proximity.

By this time, Kay and I were getting stressed out and asked our GP if anything could be done. He just suggested that she should come back for a consultation and he would try and get her to go on drugs again and go to youth talk about these sort of problems. Unfortunately she point blank refused to take drugs, although she did see the GP but again would not divulge what was said to kay or I which was frustrating for all of us.

It was at this time that Fran was spending more and more time on her laptop, late into the evening researching information about her coursework which was the American Revolution. She also spent much time watching Barack Obama on TV who was vying to become president elect of the United States around this time with the presidential vote due the following year in November 2008.

We then discovered that Fran was out shopping for strange items, such as pieces of cord, and other odd items which made no sense at all. She said it was part of her coursework but I couldn't see how that fitted in.

Several weeks later, we had a call from her school to say she had not been into assembly and not registered. She returned home later but not before we had a call from a farmer who found her near a tree with some rope and we started to fear the worst. We tried to confront Fran about this, but she covered it up and denied there was any problem, which is a trait of mental health and made it so difficult for kay and I to monitor and control this effectively.

Fran continued with her studies and coursework in the meantime, but her moods were getting noticeably darker whilst she was studying and refused to go out with friends for long periods. Instead she remained on her own but seemed happy enough in her work. However she may have been disguising a growing problem of obsessive behaviour which was becoming difficult to identify. I would watch her doing her coursework on the floor most evenings whilst watching Obama on TV in the election hustings in America at that time. She would listen to music but I could only think of 'Obsession' by Delirious reflecting the way she had become.

I was working from home, as work was slower due to the growing recession at this time so agreed with kay to watch Fran as much as possible. However I had to go out and do appointments periodically, so if Fran was working at home, it made it difficult to watch her.

The latter part of 2007 was better, and working towards her mid-term exams or AS levels in the late spring of 2008 she seemed much more settled and happier. She even started going out again with friends after a quiet period and even made some new friends at school. She also started going to guides on Monday nights and teamed up with some new contracts she would see regularly in the city, who lived near the hospital.

The weeks and months rolled by towards her AS exams, but in Easter 2008 Fran went to Washington and New York as part of her 'A' level media studies course. She was very excited about this, although we did asked her if she felt OK to go with friends and her teachers. Fortunately she went with several close friends such as Charlotte and Hannah who agreed to keep a close eye on her. They said she was OK but was a bit slow and forgetful at times on the New York subway, and had to be hurried along on occasions.

The trip was reasonable successful, with pictures of the A level group including Fran on the White House lawn, with the White House in the background. Fran also brought back a mug from the Statue of Liberty for me which was a personal present which was much treasured of course, as Fran and I had an almost telepathic relationship. I knew what she was thinking and vice versa, which is what concerned me.

By the spring of 2008 Fran had dropped many sports to concentrate on her studies, although still did rowing and squash occasionally, but still went swimming and did tennis weekly until 2009.

After the trip to America, Fran wrote up her noted and prepared for her AS levels, and was reasonably successful, exceeding the grades she had hoped for. As a celebration, the lower sixth group spent an entire day at Alton Towers enjoying themselves and Fran was in the thick of it.

She was photographed in the front seat of dare devil rides through water, on the sheer drop, rollercoaster, and every manner of scary ride -Fran was on it. Every photograph of the day had her in the front seat living every moment of excitement for all it was worth. Whilst her other friends would scream and hide, she would be in the forefront of each ride, lapping it up. She loved exhilaration as she had no fear at all. Whether it was on the rollercoaster ride, to the sound of Bon Jovi and 'It's my life,' or the water splash ride to the strains of TATU and 'All the things she said,'

Fran lived for the moment. To her there was no tomorrow. It was all about today and the here and now.

Her friends would call her 'beautiful' as she refused to be down and had no emotional baggage at all. She would light up the room when she walked in and so it was with Alton Towers, turning it into a real party day out. Needless to say they all came home late and exhausted, and rested the next day prior to the end of term.

Chapter 11 – 2008: A very challenging year.

Fran continued through 2008 and enjoyed the summer holidays and a well-earned rest after being reasonably successful in her AS levels exams in June. She spent most of the summer playing with friends over the park and spending time with her favourite nanny, Brenda who used to bring sweets and cakes which she loved. Brenda would talk in such a high pitched voice that our dog, Topaz would be alerted before she had even reached the house! You could Topaz whining as Brenda would say 'Topaz-where that dog gone?' and she would rush out to greet her for a chew.

Upon her return to studies in her final year in the upper sixth form, Fran seemed more concerned with her studies than ever. However we noted that she was starting to neglect her friends and saw them less and less which was a concern. Fran was becoming obsessed with her studies and concentrating on them, almost to the point of stopping most of her sporting activities, apart from tennis at Harpenden which she loved and would never give up.

However this obsession with her studies and particular media studies about the American Revolution and the election of Barak Obama in

November 2008 was seminal, and she focussed almost entirely on this to the exclusion of almost everything else, including her family.

Of course, we as her family tried everything to get her to talk to Youth Talk and go and see her doctor to ensure that she was OK as we worried about her. Unfortunately because of data protection laws we had no idea of what was discussed between Fran and our GP or doctor, so had no clue as to her mental state. She seemed distracted by her studies and communication was becoming more difficult in the autumn of 2008. We suspected that she was starting to have problems with psychotic complications, which was alluded to by the social workers, appointed after she ran away. We then started finding rope in her wardrobe and other alarming signs, which meant we had to start watching her more carefully and ask her where she was going when going out.

When taking her to school in the mornings she seemed more withdrawn and argumentative which was not like her. She would tell me to 'shut up dad' and turn up the radio and play her new CD, Snow Patrol-'A hundred million suns' and would play 'Engines' which was a morose track over and over again. This is classic obsessive behaviour I was informed. Talking to her in the car was also strange as she responded not like a girl but a man, which may have been her 'alter-ego' talking. The dialogue would be more masculine than feminine, and Fran took no interest in feminine things, which was a pity as she looked amazing when she dressed up, which was all too rare sadly.

Fran took an interest in the local elections when I went through the various manifestos to see which was best, although she was a year too young to vote at 17. We went through these systematically and came to a reasoned decision, which she appreciated.

She also said she would like to try learning to drive, but Kay and I thought this to be too risky as she could panic. Fran also said she didn't trust herself on the road, which sounded dangerous, so I took the decision to defer applying for a provisional licence until she finished her studies at least. This was because her brothers had had various minor accidents since passing their tests, involving scraping garden walls, misjudging corner, and hitting trees when parking. Our lovely blue Mazda 323 eventually had to be replaced due to the number of dents and repairs it had.

Then one day, we had a phone call from a farmer who said he had seen Fran with a rope near a tree on his land acting suspiciously. We then had to rush up there and collect her and ask what she was up to. She replied by playing the whole thing down but Kay and I were now getting clearly worried, we went back to the GP; specialist clinic in St. Albans and social workers, but there responses were not what we had hoped for. Instead we were told to just keep monitoring her. Fran did go and see her GP to discuss matters, but we had no feedback from either so had no idea what was happening in reality?

Several weeks went by and Fran started saying that she 'didn't fit in' and 'belonged somewhere else.' Kay was getting really worried by now and put on weight with the strain. I was working hard in the meantime, but the economy was slowing and earnings were dropping off, making the situation difficult. Family gave tacit support, including the wonderful Brenda, but she and us could only do so much. It was up to Fran to sort this problem, but we felt that's she wasn't really doing that. Instead she just concentrated on her studies to the exclusion of almost everything else. Locking herself away in her room doing coursework and watching Obama on TV in the American elections to the exclusion of virtually all else. Fran continued jogging to keep fit, but we suspected she was having Psychotic episodes by this time as she would disappear for long periods, without explanation and act mysteriously. Her friends said she seemed normal at school but was becoming withdrawn which was not like her.

On one occasion she jogged all the way to Sandridge village and back in the November mists one dark evening. We knew she was a strong runner as she could outrun James, her elder brother some 6 years older, and had tremendous stamina. She would leave the house and say she was just going out for a run to Kay. She would then walk up the road to the top of Bluehouse Hill in the mist. A passing fox's or badger's eyes would glint in the headlights of a car and reflection of the streetlights in the murky conditions.

Fran would adjust her i-pod mini which she took everywhere as music was key to Fran; and tie her running shoes before tossing her hair back and her eyes would rise up in deep concentration, before sprinting past several other runners to the tune of 'Please save me' by Sunskreem v Push, a track with dramatic resonance. She would run for hours literally, disappearing at 4pm in the winter gloom, and not return until gone 8pm when it would quite often be raining gently. Upon her return she acted like everything was normal and just return to her studies.

Fran would spend hours studying, and Kay was getting worried that she was not joining in family life at all by now. So she would go and try and talk to her, and almost plead with her to come downstairs and at least watch some TV. But Fran decided she was happy studying at length and watching Obama on TV. Clearly this was becoming an obsession, and she would continue listening to her i-pod even whilst studying and watching her TV in the background. I can imagine her listening to the haunting track 'Obsession' by Delirious? Which seemed to sum up Fran's current predicament.

Fran spent hour after hour studying and Kay and I were becoming more and more concerned. She would disappear saying she was going to the local supermarket just down the road but not come back for hours. I would challenge her when she was going out, but she covered up her actions so well, that we suspected nothing was going on. We had a report that she had been sent home from school one day after a rope was found in her locker. When challenged she said it was tie her bag, but we suspected the worst by now. She went to see her GP again but would not open up or let us into her private world. She did play tennis and go to guides though which reassured us - for the time being anyway.

Chapter 12; Fran sectioned and has a 'major psychotic attack'.

Fran one Saturday in November 2008 went out to what we thought was the shops late morning. Kay and I were cleaning at home as normal and suspected everything was normal. The boys played football Saturday morning so had gone out and we expected Fran back shortly after she had been to the supermarket to get some things for her studies and coursework, or so she said.

Imagine our surprise when 3 police officers turned up on our doorstep, and we feared the worst. Fortunately Fran was with them and they came into the lounge, where we were sitting. The police explained that Fran had been found with a rope in a public place and was suspected to be attempting to commit suicide which we found to be shocking. Clearly things were going downhill fast and this had brought things to a head. The police said she would have to be sectioned and could not release her unless it was to a social worker or she had been put into care.

Several frantic phone calls were made and her social worker from the local care home said she could either go to Stevenage, which was miles away; or the care home in St. Albans for disturbed people. We opted for the latter but the police had to accompany Fran until they had seen her formally handed over into care by a care or social worker. Fran was checked in and took her coursework books and papers with her and was taken to a small room at the back of the centre. The police left after she was checked in and she was kept in for observation for a period of 2 weeks. Obviously her school had to be informed but they were aware of the situation and were very accommodating, even allowing Fran to continue her studies in care with visits from some of her teachers, who cared greatly for her; especially the headmistress Mrs Murrell who deserves special mention as everyone's favourite former teacher at Fran's school, STAGS.

Whilst sectioned in care, Fran had visits from a number of family members to give her moral support at a trying time for all of us. After 2 weeks in care, the staff and social workers assessed Fran and came to the conclusion that she was 'sane but sad', which I thought was a strange conclusion after what had happened previously.

We did phone her GP and social worker on further occasions, but they said just watch her and check she is OK. Unfortunately we are busy people and watching her 24/7 is difficult even for 2 people as she will slip out when we are distracted by phone calls or work commitments.

We suspected that Fran had had several minor psychotic attacks or complications over the latter half of 2008, as she seemed distracted and spent long periods either in her room or at school studying on her own. Her demeanour had changed to her alter-ego of a more aggressive male character, instead of the Fran we knew and loved.

Kay suspected as much as she went swimming with Fran at Sopwell House on occasions, and on one occasion, her eyes were up in her head when Kay turned round to ask her a question which scared Kay as we didn't know how to handle this situation.

Fran would also say she was going down to the local supermarket, but spend sometimes hours out and about. One several occasions I had to go down and search the supermarket. On one occasion she was there, looking through stationery to buy and chatting to friends there for ages. On another occasion though she was nowhere to be seen. She later turned up as if nothing had happened and said she had to get some things. Is suspected she was buying rope or cord, but couldn't find it despite searching her room, as she hid things so well.

We later found a script on her computer which described Fran's fantasy world or 'secret life.' We suspect this was when she had a psychotic attack and hallucinated, not being able to discern fact from fiction or real-life events. Reading through this we found that she mentioned Michael Jackson in the room, with 'loony-toon' comic characters such as Micky Mouse, plus Star Wars characters who had strong images. They would all be in a room with her with a monkey on the ceiling. There were also descriptions of her 'alter ego,' and a distorted reality world.

We suspected that she had a major psychotic attack around mid- November 2008, as she went out and didn't come back for 3 hours, so may have become completely disorientated. When we found her she was cuddling Topaz, our Old English Sheep dog on the floor and looking around as if she was relieved we were all here, checking the room by rolling her eyes around to check the hallucinations had all gone.

A possible major attack itself must have been very frightening and nightmarish, as she would have had no control over that. The scenario would have been something like the following:-

'Fran would have walked out of the house saying she was just going down the shops to get a few things, as normal. However she was complaining of headaches and rubbing her forehead just prior to the potential psychotic attack. The attack would have been a complete audio-visual experience, taking over her controllable senses completely so she would have had little or no control over them. I would imagine a menacing soundtrack such as 30 seconds to Mars and 'Stranger in a strange land', and blurred photo-chromatic vision. In effect she was becoming a stranger in her own body.

Her vision would blend to monochromatic images before becoming infra-red and panning into multiple images into the distance, giving a distorted view of events. Fran would then be projected into a virtual room with characters such as Michael Jackson, plus comic characters such as Micky Mouse, Goofy and Star wars Characters and a monkey and Chinese man on the ceiling which she mentioned in her computer blogs and English stories she wrote for school.

This would give way to her standing by a busy road watching cars go by with lights streamed past in slow motion timing, giving a banner effect whilst her eyes by this time would be in her head struggling to comprehend these images.

This would merge to a mountain top where her alter ego would disseminate and materialise in front of her as a young man, at odds with her in her own body, pictured wearing illuminated glasses. A struggle would ensue between Fran and her alter ego for control of her mind. Knowing Fran, she would have put up a determined struggle, but may been pushed backwards, falling into space, and ending up against a backdrop of Andromeda, lost in time and space and feeling helpless, slowly losing control of her mind and conscious faculties during this period.

She would later awake cuddling Topaz, our sheep dog not knowing how or why she had ended up there, after leaving the house to go shopping. Strangest of all was that she couldn't remember any of this in her conscious mind? This is something that affects the subconscious mind and is not completely understood even today.'

I suggested to Fran that she try an electro-magnetic therapy device known as a 'Magnetech' to see if that would improve things, but again she would refuse any kind of medication or help on principle as she liked to do things and make decisions for herself.

After the attack and time in care Fran talked about her future, and said she would like to try and emulate her elder brother Christian which was at University studying to be lawyer, which he later successfully became. Fran also talked about working for Charity abroad and doing community work, but I said that the world was becoming a dangerous place these days. However Kay and I were becoming increasingly fearful for Francesca's future, which was looking more and more unlikely as she worked towards her final exams in June 2009, with mock exams in January 2009.

Again she would be working alone in her room with her i-pod glued to her ear whilst watching Obama on TV celebrating his win in the US presidential election. Fran would be rejecting offers to go out with friends though, which we thought was unhealthy and said she should go out more. Instead, she carried on studying to the strains of Savage Garden and 'Crash and Burn;' plus the Editors and other 'Indie' bands such as the Killers and Snow Patrol, her favourite band.

Fran rarely dressed up, but made an exception for a friend's party on New Year's Eve in 2008. She agreed under some peer pressure from Charlotte and several of her friends to get made up in her room with several friends helping her, and selecting clothes for the occasion. They spent one Saturday morning dressing her up for the party, and when finished she looked a million dollars.

I later dropped her off with several friends, and picked them up after mid-night. They went to a house party in St. Albans with a number of her girlfriends and some guys and had a great time. Some of the guys were pictured with her and said, like the Script song, 'Never seen anything quite like you' and where have you been all this time? I suspect studying far too much. I was chuffed though when Fran was the first to send me a text message after midnight on January 1st saying 'Happy New Year dad'. A priceless moment from one who really cared.

After the New Year's Eve party, Fran knuckled down to her studies and seemed more focussed, concentrating on her mock A levels in January where she seemed quite normal and getting on with her life. On her way to school she was much focussed and spent most of her time engrossed in her studies. I tried talking to her but occasionally her alter ego would respond and seemed quite curt and rude, almost like a man at times and not like Fran at all. On the way to school and back in the car she would listen to her CD and turn off Absolute Radio I was listening to without even asking. I tried discussing things with her but it was becoming hard work, as seemed to only be interested in her studies rather than spending time with friends or on hobbies, which seemed unhealthy.

Chapter 13; 2009; Fran's untimely demise.

As we moved into 2009, the economy was getting worse and although I and Kay continued working, it was a struggle keeping going and making ends meet. Fran's brothers, James and Adam were still living at home but spending much time away, with James completing his legal qualifications and Adam planning a move to Sandridge in rented accommodation nearby with his girlfriend Holly, whom we saw often. Holly was a veterinary nurse and loved our Old English Sheep dog, Topaz.

The weeks rolled by and Fran was studying hard. I actually spent time with her going through the options for her Media studies coursework, where she had to discuss the manifestos for the upcoming elections in 2009 and 2010, where she would be old enough to vote. Fran also talked about learning to drive, but Kay and I poured cold water on that idea, given recent events by saying perhaps do that after her exams, and get those out of the way first?

As we entered early April, we had an unseasonal cold snap of wintery weather, with several inches of snow. Fran of course loved this, which proved a nice distraction from the endless hours of studying she was putting in. I also helped her with her History coursework where she was studying Obama's recent election as president and looking at American presidential history, which was quite interesting going through all the previous presidents and what they did.

Several of Fran's friends encouraged her to spend a day in the park playing in the snow, and provided some nice photos of them throwing snowballs and messing about in a deserted park covered in snow. The lake in the park was also frozen with ducks skating across the ice, and Swans and Moorhens looking distinctly out of place on the bank.

The discussions with our GP continued but frustratingly neither Fran or our GP would discuss what was said due to data protection regulations, which we found infuriating and may eventually led to her demise as we did not know what was really happening and had little warning. The GP just said keep an eye on her and the social workers likewise, but we felt like this was not really addressing the problem. I did suggest to Kay that we should pay for a clinical psychologist to assess Fran, but couldn't really afford it at that time. We also both had to work because of the recession, which didn't help matters.

April 19th rolled around and we celebrated Fran's coming of age with a party. She dressed up for the occasion with a little help from Charlotte and her friends and we all went out to a Chinese restaurant in Harpenden which was nice evening. One of Fran's nannies made a 'handbag' cake, and all the immediate family attended, including Aunt Pam and Brenda; along with Claire, Fran's cousin who was 17 at that time and most of my family.

Fran's birthday was actually on the Sunday, and I took her to Harpenden again instead of doing archery, to meet her friend who failed to turn up sadly. After a phone call though, one of her male friends turned up and they went to the pub for a drink, which she could now do legally on her own.

The afternoon was spent giving blood at a hotel in London Road, St. Albans although we had to wait what seemed like ages to give blood and then wait in the recovery area. However Fran was adamant that that was what she wanted to do on her birthday-always thinking of others less fortunate than her.

That evening Kay and I had booked to go away for our 25th wedding anniversary in Dubai, so left Fran and the boys in the capable hands of Brenda at our place late afternoon whilst we headed out for the airport.

I felt a bit sad going away at that time, as Fran needed as much support as she could get really. I was therefore very surprised and honoured to receive a text from Fran whilst in the toilets at Heathrow saying have a great holiday Dad and Happy Anniversary to you and Mum.

Our week away was a much needed break when we appreciated it, not knowing of the trauma about to come. Kay and I recharged our batteries, and spent time looking at the giant aquariums in Dubai in the shopping malls, surprised that many of the shops had English or American brand names. The weather was hot even for April and we ate outdoors even at night, although the sun seems to set there at 6pm all year round. It was also strange that Friday was a day of rest and Sunday was a working day.

We returned to the UK to find that the boys and Fran enjoyed having Brenda for a week, and commented that they enjoyed the cooked breakfasts, sweets, and goodies that Nanny would buy in large quantities, together with dog treats that kept Topaz, our Old English sheepdog, busy.

April became May and Fran by this time was revising frantically for her exams. We were obviously a little concerned about the pressure she was under but she gave no clue of being in distress or being under undue pressure. I took her to nearby Hatfield University library in late May for a final revision session and she seemed fine, looking up references for items likely to come up in her exams.

In the car on the way back she suddenly opened up about what she would like to do once she finished her exams and would like to go onto University. She also talked about doing charity work abroad, although I said that could be dangerous for a single girl given the war in Afghanistan that was raging at that time. She also talked about doing charity work in Africa and perhaps becoming a legal executive like her elder brother, James who was completing his qualification as a lawyer around that time.

The month of June arrived and Fran commenced her final exams with trepidation. We were obviously anxious, but she seemed OK to start off with. I picked her up and we discussed how things went and if she wanted any help, but she seemed OK. She did go out a fair bit, saying she needed more pencils, rubbers, ink, etc. although we don't know if that was true or not. Half way through her exams, the family were due to go down to Burnham on Crouch for a family party, as Uncle Gordon was celebrating his 80th birthday. We all went to a restaurant overlooking the river, but Fran said she wanted to stay at home all day with Topaz and revise. Kay and I discussed this with Brenda and we said OK, as she seemed fine with no signs of any outward distress, despite previous events. So we went off to Burnham, but alerted our neighbour Roz and Geoff, and also my parents who were nearby in case of any problems. We also gave Fran our mobile numbers and said ring if there are any problems. Well the day went without a hitch, and we returned to find Fran still studying in the early evening.

Fran's last 2 exams were more spread out over 2 weeks, as the rest were together in the first 2 weeks of June. This meant she had a long time to revise for just one exam at a time. Fran started to become more remote in those last 2 weeks, and spent time trying to go out and avoid us. She also spent much time jogging to keep fit and went swimming for long periods at Cannons, on one occasion up to 6 hours such was her determination and single mindedness. I can imagine her now, swimming to the strains of 'Breathing Underwater' by Metric. However it may have been due to her illness. In the car during those last two exams, she seemed more argumentative as her alter ego came through increasingly, and we were slowly losing our daughter to something we did not recognise that was bigger than all of us.

When all the exams were finished there was obviously much celebrating with friends, who went out for drinks and an end of school party, taking loads of photographs, and celebrating one of the girls birthdays. I think it was Lauren's from memory with photos of Fran drinking from a bottle leaning against Lauren who was smiling with silver balloons and bunting and cards in the background.

Fran's last week of term and final week was busy, as her friends had organised a whole series of events. This included a trip to see Darren Brown in London on the Wednesday, with photographs of all of the girls on the Charing Cross Northern Line platform dressed for the occasion. Fran enjoyed this immensely as she loved illusions and playing tricks. Fran also went to Wimbledon on the Thursday and spent a day in the outer courts watching matches and having picnics in the sun. Fran had her customary Egg fried rice in a plastic box, but was pulling faces when photographed and grimaced for what should have been a nice picture in her new Aegon blue tennis top which she only wore several times. Her friends also went to the park to play on the swings and also the cinema with her.

On the Thursday, Fran went with kay to Sopwell to have a spa day by the pool, and have a manicure and girls day out after the stress of her exams. However whilst swimming, Kay went to wave to Fran and noticed that she didn't look quite right. Kay asked if Fran was alright on her return but Fran said she felt fine. The problem is she probably didn't even remember what happened at all or was even aware of it?

On the Friday, Fran spent the entire day with one of her friends, Mikki, who came round and they went out and had a nice day at the pub, where her friend worked, before going up to the city centre to window shop. They spent the day laughing and chatting before returning home in the evening and Mikki said Fran was fine, when Kay asked how she was.

The following day, Saturday 27th June 2009 started brightly with bright warm sunshine and we all awoke early. It was day to remember for all the wrong reasons. Fran seemed agitated that day as if she was planning something but we couldn't work out what. Kay searched her wardrobe and couldn't find anything because of all her course notes. In view of what happened on the Thursday, we said to the boys who were at home not to all go out together leaving Fran on her own, if we had to go out.

Fran threw me a packet of chocolates to me sat in the garden from her window which she didn't want which was unusual, as she loved chocolate. She also was having a clear out of her room that day. We stayed in but said we would be taking Topaz out at 12.30 for about 40 minutes around the park, but one of the boys would probably be around. Anyway, Kay and I went to take Topaz out, thinking James or Adam were in to keep an eye on her. Unfortunately, James had gone to Watford, and Adam and Holly went to look at a rented place in Sandridge locally. We went out thinking someone was in.

So for just 40 minutes the house was empty, but that was all it took. We returned and sensed something was wrong as it seemed eerily quiet for a Saturday with several birds squabbling outside our house, and I sensed something wasn't right immediately. I immediately rushed inside and shouted Fran, but there was no response. I rushed upstairs and her door was locked from the inside. I raced to the garage to get a ladder to see if I get in from the outside, but her blind was drawn and the window locked.

We called the emergency services and the police arrived within 5 minutes, the ambulance and fire brigade took longer though, arriving about 13.20-25. Realising that time could be crucial we asked the fireman to break down her door. So we stood clear whilst he anchored himself against the stairs and gave the door several hard kicks. It took several minutes before the door opened and revealed a horrible sight. Fran was prostrate hanging from the light fitting with curtain cord of all things. I cut her down and laid her on the landing floor so the paramedics could administer CPR. They managed to get a heartbeat and keep her alive, but the delay meant that she was probably brain dead already.

Fran's floor was covered in urine, and she was wearing her pink T shirt and combat trousers and trainers I recall. After what seemed an eternity, the ambulance left for the hospital. Unfortunately it was a Saturday afternoon so the roads were busy, so it took till nearly 15.00 to reach Accident and Emergency. There we checked in and waited what seemed ages.

But were not allowed to see her whilst she was in a coma.

I had to ring James and Adam to tell them what had happened. Unfortunately Brenda was away with Terry, her partner on a cruise. After some discussions with the family, we decided not to try and contact her as she was at sea, and didn't want to ruin her holiday. I also informed my parents but they took longer to arrive, along with my sister Kim and her husband.

Eventually we were allowed in to see Fran who was lying prostrate on the bed in accident and emergency. What surprised us was the number of young people in there who had been involved in road accidents whilst distracted by iPods, etc. or taken drugs and had a reaction and were in a coma. Kay and I stayed overnight as we didn't know if Fran would survive the night. However she stabilised and seemed better on the Sunday. Relatives came and visited on the Sunday and Monday and I asked if I could use my magnetic therapy device but the medical staff said no initially. I looked at Fran's charts and monitors, and although her heart and lungs were working well on life support, the doctors were surprisingly gloomy, saying that all her other organs were effectively dead.

We were taken into a room with my mum and dad and Kim and her husband, by the doctor and transplant surgeon. It was there that they said Fran's chances of survival were almost nil, and that she would die and they wanted to turn off the life support machine. This initially horrified kay and me.

We were then asked for consent to allow Fran's organs to be transplanted, in the presence of other family and with no prior warning at all. I said to Kay that all of Fran's organs effectively died on the Saturday with only her heart and lungs remaining on life support. Fran would have readily supported donating her organs to save a life, but in this case I felt it was already too little, too late. So Kay and I decided to decline consent.

We spent the Monday hoping against hope that our wonderful Fran could survive, as she was such an amazing person inside and out. That was not me saying that - her friends and people she met say she was exceptional in taking care of people and considering others first. That is something this world so badly lacks these days. Fran also had no fears or emotional baggage like so many people. She lived for the moment as perhaps she realised and knew that her time here was limited so she had to make the most of it and leave a lasting legacy.

On the Monday 29th, we stayed with Fran and although there was some slight movement of her lips, she never really regained consciousness. I pleaded with the medical staff to be able to use my Magnetech magnetic therapy device, and they eventually relented on the basis that Fran was effectively a lost cause.

I did try using the Magnetech against Fran's head for 20 minutes, and noted her condition seemed to improve temporarily. However this was a last gasp attempt to save our daughter, as she had probably suffered severe brain damage by the time we reached her. I continued to apply the Magnetech to give Fran some comfort in her final moments, but the medical staff said it was probably futile. During Monday evening we had a family crisis meeting in the hospital as we realised that things would not be the same after this. We also had to talk to the medical staff about what happens next in this kind of event, which is not always straightforward.

I watched as Fran just lay there on the bed looking out the window towards the west with her picture with her brothers at the end of her bed and small teddies on her pillow to keep her company. The nurses went to and fro, watching the monitors and keeping an eye on things, but her organ traces had flat lined. Her heartbeat and breathing seemed OK.

On Tuesday 30th June 2009, we met the doctors and had the news we were dreading. They said that Fran was being kept alive by life support machine and they wanted to turn this off. Clearly this was a huge decision but we felt we had little real choice in practice. We reviewed all the evidence and very reluctantly Kay and I agreed that the life support machine could be switched off and Fran allowed to slip away quietly.

That was at 16.30, and she had gone by 16.50. However she survived 20 minutes simply because she was so physically fit. If it wasn't for the ASF, she was the strongest person I have ever known, both physically and mentally. I remember going into the lift lobby and staring up at the heavens and praying and asking God, 'why are you doing this to us'? Other people don't have this hurt and level of suffering, although I have since learned that many families have lost nearest and dearest in circumstances they didn't expect to lose.

What is most frustrating is that the people we depend on and are a key part of our lives are always the ones that are taken first. Over the years I feel like I have lost a large part of my immediate support 'team' leaving me personally isolated. The people like Fran who were always there for you and would do anything for you, snatched from this world before you can even say goodbye.

The last 20 minutes of Fran's life was a form of Chinese torture. From 16.30 to 16.50, I paced up and down watching the monitors after the life support machine was turned off. The lights kept flashing and nurses ignored them, attending to other patients. I looked through the doctors charts but all Fran's organs had flat lined bar 2, meaning they were dead. The rest of the family hugged Fran as she lay motionless, and a priest summoned by my Mum administered the last rights. Fran deserved better than this.

The nurses continued to walk past and drew the curtains and put up a privacy notice. It was at this point I imagined Pink Floyd's 'Comfortably numb' to be appropriate, and walked off to an area at the rear to vent my frustration with this completely unacceptable situation. In what I call a slow motion 'silent scream,' I thumped the table, sending a Coke can flying and punched through a stud wall. I then crouched with clenched fists venting my fury with God, with tears in my eyes but an overwhelming determination to realise Fran's legacy after what had happened.

The end was an anti-climax, and 2 nurses simply pulled a sheet across Fran's head to bring to an end a remarkable 18 year love story and an unforgettable life. Fran had had her problems, but she also was here for a reason. Aunt Gilly had told me a wonderful story that before Fran was born and just after Colin, Brenda's husband had died back in July 1990 just before she was born; that Fran had asked about joining our family whilst in heaven. It seemed that this was pre-destined? It also seems that Fran wanted to join our family, as she once gave me a Father's Day tablet that said simply 'If all the fathers of the world were hands held in friendship, yours is the one I would hold.'

We collected our things and made our weary way home and spent a few days letting the dust settle and making arrangements. The fact that Fran died unnaturally meant that there had to be an inquest. Fortunately, they agreed that a post mortem wasn't necessary as I don't think I could have faced that. We had to register the death and make arrangements for the funeral. Fran's body was left in the mortuary at the hospital before being released to the undertakers. Flowers and messages of support flooded in but what surprised us was the reaction on social media, and notices in the press we knew nothing about.

Several eerie things happened straight after Fran died. A small white feather floated down onto 'Bundles,' one of her favourite teddies which is now centre stage on our bed. The other was Laura whom she is buried with, as she had from a very early age and took her everywhere. Several days later a huge dark coloured butterfly flew through the house from the lounge, up the stairs and into Adam's room before leaving via the window. This was no ordinary butterfly as it was huge, and looked like a small bird.

Organising the funeral was more complex than we thought. Kay and I met our local vicar who agreed to host the funeral, but an old friend also agreed to read the address who is now a vicar in Kent. He kindly agreed to come up for the day, and meet old friends including my brother Mike who he knew from school days. The funeral though was delayed as the body was not released for the best part of 2 weeks.

I was advised to keep working to take my mind off of what happened. To some extent it worked, although I remember surveying a house in Hemel Hempstead the Thursday after and thinking 'what am I doing here? For the first 3 months we were in a daze, and were offered counselling as a family. This we took up and had a meeting with John Hale who came highly recommended for cases involving young suicides, as his own brother had done the same, we understand.

Chapter 14; Fran's Funeral and Wake

The funeral was eventually agreed for Friday 17th July 2009. The Tuesday before, we were given an opportunity to view the body whilst 'lying in state.' When we saw Fran, Brenda immediately remarked 'that's not the Fran I know.' Fran had been dead 3 weeks and although her skin was good, and she was dressed all in black with trousers, top and cardigan but no shoes. We had concerns about the coffin which was English Oak with brass handles and plaque, but the internal lining was plastic, so we asked for that to be improved. There was a thin mark around Fran's neck where the ligature had been, but she was at peace now. Brenda and Kay went again to view the body on the Thursday prior to the funeral but I couldn't face it again.

The day of the funeral was bright but showery. Plenty of flowers were delivered and many of our friends and work colleagues were genuinely shocked by what had happened, as it seemed so out of character for Fran. The flowers were arranged along our patio in a line but there were loads of them. Many were from her school friends who mourned her loss personally. Several girls had died at her school, but we didn't expect her to be one of them. One had died at 14 from sudden death syndrome which is awful, as there is no warning. Another had taken her own life coping with the pressures of exams. Another has since died shortly after Fran's death.

The family turned up for the funeral which was scheduled for 2pm at St. Stephen's church nearby. The limousines and hearse turned up and the family climbed aboard. We drove slowly to the church, and it seemed strange looking at places you know in a different light. The limousine and hearse pulled into the churchyard and we alighted and walked slowly into the church.

The church was filled with 150 people, many of them her school friends sobbing and weeping, plus friends from her sports clubs including archery, tennis, etc. and wider family and friends, including guides which she had attended as a teenager. We entered to the sound of the Killers and 'Human' which was one of Fran's recent album acquisitions. The vicar then gave the address and the sad circumstances of Fran's untimely demise. We then sang several Hymns the family had agreed, prior to the addresses.

Speeches and tributes were given by myself as Fran's father, James her eldest brother, and her former headmistress, Mrs Murrell. A reading was also given by Seth, a former friend and vicar from Kent, a former school friend of my brother, Mike.

I gave the main funeral address which went as follows;

FRANCESCA LAURA SPELZINI
19th April 1991- 30th June 2009

Welcome to St. Stephens today and we are pleased to see so many of Francesca's family and friends here today;

particularly the Reverend Seth Cooper who is an old family friend who has travelled up from Kent; plus my aunts, Mary and Helen, who have flown in specially from Ireland to be here today to help in this celebration of Francesca's life.

Any loss of life is sad, but loss of such a young vibrant life is tragic, and the house feels so empty without her as if she has gone away for a long holiday. Francesca's mobile was jammed full of numbers of family and friends, and she had her own Facebook page, email, and MSN messenger accounts and was always selfless, putting others first. A remembrance page set up on Facebook; titled 'In memory of Francesca Spelzini,' now has 194 group contacts world-wide, and has provided many recent photos and tributes.

There will be a retiring collection for the Asperger's Syndrome Foundation at the back of the church, and there will also be an inquest into her death, plus a remembrance service at STAGS on Tuesday 1st September at 2pm for the family and upper sixth of 2009. I must also thank the emergency services who gave us 3 more precious days with our daughter to say goodbye in our own time which has helped enormously.

Francesca was a loving and caring free spirit and was more of a tomboy than a 'girly girl,' preferring combat trousers and tee shirts to dresses and make up, which was a pity as she looked lovely on the rare occasions when she did dress up. Snow Patrol were her favourite band, but she also liked the Killers, the Fratellis, the Kooks, the Script, etc. and indeed had tickets to see Franz Ferdinand this autumn. She also supported fair trade, was a registered blood donor, supported green policies and was obsessed with sport.

Like any typical teenager she had her moments, and was thrown out of the school library for chatting too loudly, and offered her size 7 shoes to a friend when she had blisters even though she was a size 5. She also offered to walk home when all her friends couldn't fit in the car, and gave a beggar her last 10 dollars whilst on holiday in Vancouver. I once asked her what the best day of her life was, and without hesitating said a day out whilst on holiday at the chocolate factory at Broc in Switzerland.

Francesca was born on a Friday night on 19th April 1991 at 2250 at QE2 hospital at Welwyn Garden City, and spent her early years at Prae-Wood playgroup. She then moved on to St. Michael's Primary School before going briefly to Harpenden Prep school, and moved to Stormont junior girls' School in Potters Bar where she blossomed. She later successfully gained entry to St. Albans Girls School where she was until recently.

The happiest and most successful part of her all too brief life, was arguably the period from 10-16 years of age when she excelled in a variety of sports, including skiing and snowboarding, and was a very strong swimmer from an early age and won a series of swimming certificates in her last year; plus a book prize on dogs for the 'best achiever' in her final year at Stormont school. She also regularly took part in school hockey, netball, and swimming competitions at this time.

At age 11, she started STAGS and loved it immediately. She also joined Abbey Bowmen of St. Albans and quickly followed in her Dad's footsteps in winning the GNAS national gold medal in 2002. She went on to become a key part of Abbey's junior Recurve team over 5 years and in 2003 she was part of Abbey's winning team. In 2004 Francesca went to the Hertford Junior fun shoot and came first in the Recurve, second in Barebow and won the Lady Paramount' s prize and her heart. The following year she came second in the Recurve event, but later concentrated on her GCSE's and 'A' levels. Francesca was also a member of Broxbourne rowing club, 'Top golf' at Watford, and the former Cannons Health club where she did squash, swimming, running and keep fit; but her favourite sport was tennis, plus she also did Badminton at Harpenden Leisure centre.

We made a key decision to have 3 children early in our married lives, so that we would remain young parents and have many happy memories rather than regrets. In Francesca's case this meant a number of holidays to the Lake District, Cornwall, Italy, France, Belgium, Switzerland, and Canada; plus New York and Washington covering the American elections with STAGS as she loved government and politics, and she was given full support from her family and friends in all that she did.

Sadly, we shall not be able to see our daughter realise her full potential, but feel confident that she would have gained sufficient grades to go onto University and getting her results this August will be difficult. However in just 18 years she already achieved more than some achieve in 80. We were also pleased that she reached her legal majority and enjoyed a number of key family events in recent years; such as her grandparents' golden wedding, her parents' silver wedding, her aunt's 80th birthday plus her nanny's 70th and 80th birthdays and her father's 50th birthday, plus her own 18th birthday of course.

It is hoped that Francesca's life will be commemorated in a number of positive ways: Firstly, STAGS are considering an annual 'Fran cup' for the best achiever in tennis, and may also name a tree, bench, or sports facility in her memory. Secondly, it may be possible to name a junior archery event in her name, as she was the first junior girl to achieve a Barebow single clout record in Herts, which still stands. Finally, after sorting through her possessions and contact with her many friends recently; we have found numerous recent photos, a Tae Kwondo licence and other sporting medals and certificates. It is hoped that these can be brought together in time to form a comprehensive record of Francesca's brief but eventful life.

We have already had requests from relatives in Ireland and Australia for copies of photos and a resume of her achievements, and who have kindly arranged prayers and services in her memory.

With her infectious smile that lit up any room, zany sense of humour and happy go lucky approach to life, plus an inner natural beauty and concern about global warming and social injustice, Francesca has set an example to us all. In our eyes she will remain forever young and free and she is now at peace.

She leaves behind her father, Paul; her mother Kay, and brothers James, 24; and Adam, 22 plus Topaz, her much adored sheepdog. God bless you Francesca - it was a privilege and an honour to have been blessed with such a special daughter as part of our family for 18 precious years which we will surely treasure, and no doubt one day we will meet again?

Paul and Kay Spelzini - 16th July 2009

Delivering the speech was hard, as I suddenly realised half way through that Fran really had really gone for good, and had to pause briefly and re-group.

We then sang several hymns including 'Jerusalem;' an old favourite of Colin's suggested by Brenda; 'Turn, turn, turn' from the book of Ecclesiasts and 'Channel of my peace.'

Her brothers both gave addresses along with the Reverend Seth Cooper and David Ridgeway, Fran's local priest. A special address was given by her Headmistress, Mrs Mundell, who gave Fran a glowing report and said she was one of the few girls who took the time and trouble to thank all her teachers at the end of the 6th form exams for all their support. I remember she said she wore chocolate coloured shoes in memory of Fran's love of confectionary and crisps.

The pall bearers than collected the coffin that was taken out of the church to Fran's final resting place, in the centre of the churchyard on the north side. Befittingly it was a sunny location, like her personality and we walked out of the church to perhaps Fran's most favoured and moving song - Snow Patrol's 'Chasing Cars.'

Outside the church the mourners slowly gathered and paid tribute to Fran and also expressed sorrow to family members. Adam, I remember threw a rose onto the coffin and some dirt and simply said 'Bye Fran.' I threw a red English long stem rose and privately thought she was the simply best thing that had happened to me, before or since. James stood in silence, and work colleagues came by one by one, and members of her archery club including her friends Mary, Lucy, and Katherine to pay condolences, followed by her friends and former school mates.

We made our way back home to conduct the wake, where the mourners and family gathered and we had tea and discussed the day. Seth who had kindly come up from Kent stayed briefly, but left early to get back to Walmer on the south coast where he now lives and is the local vicar.

I spent time talking to Mary and Helen, my cousins who had come over from Ireland to catch up with them and recent family events since we last met around 2004 with Aunt Eileen in Australia who came over when Fran was 13 at my parents' house.

Flowers were arranged in a line along the edge of the patio lying on the grass and made quite a sight as there were so many. We also had loads of Facebook messages, letters, and cards to open, so it took a while. The family stayed for what seem like ages but Kay and I just wanted to mourn in private, although Fran's friends stayed for a while longer. The weather wasn't great I recall with frequent showers all day and during the funeral as it was humid.

When it was all over, most people had left and it was just Myself, Kay and Brenda plus the boys, James and Adam and their girlfriends remaining, as they still lived at home then. However they went out later on to leave us in peace. That gave Kay, Brenda, and I time to reflect how the day went and more importantly where we went from here. We still had an inquest to attend and some formalities to attend to.

The days passed after the funeral but work was slow. Kay took several weeks off but decided to return to work to take her mind off things, but work was quiet as the economy was struggling. I remember doing a Building Survey in Hemel Hempstead the Thursday after the funeral and thinking 'what am I doing here'?

I was spending a number of days working from home at this stage, and helped Kay with walking Topaz, our dog and doing household chores as the boys still lived at home then, although were looking to move out. Whilst taking Topaz around the field near us, I started to notice tiny white feathers float down near me, and this happened on a number of occasions. I mentioned this to Brenda and she said with no hesitation that that was a sign from Fran.

The days turned into weeks and we started seeing John Hale, on the recommendation of our GP, as he was a trauma counsellor dealing with suicides as we understand that his own brother did something similar. He insisted on seeing us shortly after the funeral and at regular intervals but insisted we all attend, that being Myself Kay, James, and Adam.

We attended the first session, but the boys were quite argumentative which surprised me. Adam was angry at what Fran had done, whilst James tried to blame us for this situation which I found puzzling. However, the counsellor was particularly good and said that we would all have feelings of guilt, grief and anger and frustration at various times over the coming months, and it would take several years for these to subside.

We had a number of these sessions at the local clinic over several years until we felt that they had served their purposes and the boys wanted to move on. However it was useful talking around the subject, although for me personally it was difficult as I was the one most intimately involved in Fran's life so arguably the one most affected by her loss?

Chapter 15; Events after Fran's funeral

A surprising suggestion was one made by Brenda, who regularly rang Aunt Gilly who lived on the south coast with her family. We had been down to visit Uncle Ray and his wife Sheila in nearby Bexhill-on-Sea for a day out with Chris, Kay's brother and family around that time; and it was she who suggested that Brenda, Kay and I should come down to the south coast for a healing session. At first I didn't take this seriously, but Brenda convinced us to spend a day on the south coast and talk about things generally, whilst having a healing session. Gilly was a trained healer and therapist and was deeply knowledgeable about these matters.

So Kay, Brenda and I took a day out of our schedule and drove around the M25 and down the A20 to Hastings and St. Leonards, where she lived then. Gilly has since moved to Leominster with her partner. We were lucky to pick a sunny day and turned up at her bungalow with splendid views across the bay and watched the trains pulling up at St. Leonard's station below us, as we were on a hill.

We obviously discussed what had happened and Gilly had come to our house shortly after the funeral at her suggestion to assist with the healing process. She said that Fran was indeed with us in spirit whilst we were talking and I felt a freezing cold sensation whilst sitting on the settee. She said that Fran could sense what we were saying and even smell scents, as Gilly said that Francesca had noticed that Kay had changed her perfume?

We also discussed Colin which Brenda was obviously interested in as her former partner who passed on in 1990. Gilly said to look out for feathers, as we and Brenda had been getting them, sometimes without realising it, letting us know of Fran's spiritual presence.

Gilly then suggested that we both have a healing session to reduce stress. This involved going into a darkened room and lying down. Gilly would then draw up 'stress' through the top of the head and administer some relaxing oils, whilst administering healing therapy. This was to help Kay and me who had been under a lot of pressure at that time, both in terms of the loss of Fran and the struggling economy at that time.

In other areas, a number of comments were made by Fran's friends and family in the months after her death. These included a celebration of her life to be held at her former school, STAGS in the September of 2009. This was three months after her death and I was asked to give a brief address, along with several others. This was organised by her school and friends, so we were a little surprised to see that my parents and my sister and partner had invited themselves along without our knowledge.

The school had mounted a vinyl plaque with a small tree in the school's commemorative garden, the base of which was overlain with flowers. Since then the area has been covered by bark chippings and made into a seating area for quiet reflection.

Fran's archery club used to shoot there in the winter months until 2013, but have since moved to Sandringham School, and many of her friends are no longer at the club. The parents of one of Fran's archery friends, Mary, kindly agreed to provide a silver platter as a trophy to be shot for by juniors each year, and named in Fran's memory which was a nice gesture. For the first few years this was open to all comers and shot in late May at the sandpit lane field. However since 2013, it is now included in the Abbey junior shoot which is now indoors and held every March.

Fran's former school, STAGS, agreed to present an annual tennis trophy in her name and asked if we wanted it presented as a team trophy or individual trophy? Kay and I decided that an individual trophy was more personal and would be awarded to the best improved tennis player over the academic year, as Fran herself was quite a player by all accounts and a thoroughly modern girl.

I remember having to procure a trophy in autumn of 2009, so went about searching the internet for suitable tennis trophies. Initially these were quite predictable with silver cups or platters, but I wanted something a little more unique but modern to reflect Fran's unique character. After ploughing through pages of cups, shields, and platters, I came across a website with tennis trophies made to order. One featured a depiction of a girl serving cut into a glass block by a laser, and mounted on a simple square base at a sensible price. So that was that.

The trophy when it arrived in the post was a delight. It sparkled in the sunlight reminding me of Fran and although quite small, was inspirational which a trophy should be. I presented the trophy the first few times, but Kim my sister obliged and stood in for me several times, as I was away or couldn't make some dates. I understand that the school have now erected a list of previous winners in the main school hall which I would like to see as I haven't seen it yet? I would imagine the Script's 'Hall of Fame' would be appropriate as a soundtrack to the presentation of Frans' trophies, sparkling as they do in the bright sunlight during May and July when they were presented originally.

Fran's grave was marked by a temporary timber marker until January 2010. That winter was quite cold with snow, so her grave was covered by a blanket of snow for some weeks. Her friends and family would leave flowers regularly, although the frequency of flowers being left has gradually declined over the years as people have moved on with their lives. A permanent gravestone in granite was erected in January 2010 which we went to see and approve in a barn on the A4146 in December 2009 prior to installation.

Chapter 16; Fran's Legacy and finding a cure for Mental Health issues?

Fran's immediate legacy includes her archery platter which continues to be awarded every March at Abbey Bowmen, her former club at the Edge Grove junior tournament. This also includes the Peter Newbery trophy who was the Chairman of Abbey Bowmen during much of Fran's membership there, and during which time both Abbey and Fran bloomed in terms of numbers of trophies won and recognition. Arguably that was the most successful period the club had ever experienced since its formation in 1968, and has relapsed somewhat since then into a more settled existence with new people coming in and a number old familiar faces since departed.

Fran's former school continue to award her splendid tennis trophy every July at the end of the summer term to the most promising tennis player over the academic year. A list of the winners is now proudly displayed in the main hall, along with other award winners and will ensure that Fran's name is not forgotten. I can imagine the presentation along to the strains of the Script and 'Hall of Fame,' because that is where Fran deserved to be with her numerous sporting capabilities. The trophies glinting and sparkling in the sunlight reminded me of her sparkling attitude to sport and also giving people a chance. She once said that she would sometimes let the youngsters whom she played against in squash and tennis on a Saturday win, as she didn't want to discourage them if she played at full power which she was certainly capable of, as confirmed by her tennis friends.

Fran's longer term legacy is more complex and would involve tackling the thorny question of mental Health issues worldwide. 1 in 4 people now suffer mental health issues at some stage in their lives - usually as a result of stress or worries about money and relationships. There is no easy solution here as every case is different.

Cancer affects 1 in 3 people worldwide and tends to get more media coverage, as there are medical advances and this can be treated physically by surgery and modern drugs. Mental health is different as you cannot simply operate or use drugs to cure a mental health problem, as mental health is in the mind or brain which has complex electro-synaptic links to the central nervous system. The current favoured treatment seems to be use drugs to dull the symptoms and sedate people, so that the symptoms can be controlled more easily. However that is not a long term cure.

Some genetic therapies seem to have worked to a limited extent to reduce the risk of offspring having recurrent mental health issues, but that is of little comfort to people already suffering from current mental health problems. Many mental health issues are literally in the mind.

Perhaps what we need is a whole different approach to mental health, as mental health should be treated using a non-invasive procedures. It is here that we look to the future and a futuristic 'Star-Trek' type medical solution such as the Magnetech. This is an electrical wand that rotates at high speed generating an electro-magnetic field. The tip of the wand is placed on the part of the body requiring treatment, usually the head or brain for a limited period to bring relief to the patient.

The Magnetch can be used for other ailments including hearing problems and physical injury to speed up healing times for sportsman, where time lost can be expensive. However its real advantage is treating parts of the body, such as the brain that are too delicate for normal surgery. It can also be used once a week for a general tune up of health for older people and helps them relax. This can be done by holding the wand with the fingers of both hands for just 5 minutes a week. This gives a tingling sensation in the hands and stimulates the body's own immune system to speed healing and help relax the patient.

Too many young girls like Fran get to late teenage years, which is the highest risk area for depression and suicidal thoughts without real help. Talking is the simplest remedy, but Fran would not talk to Youth talk or discuss her issues as she would disguise them and say she had no problem, simply covering it up. That is the hardest thing to deal with where people are simply in denial that they have a problem or simply ignore it, which can be dangerous as in Fran's case.

Since Fran's passing, Brenda was an essential support for 4 years before her eventual demise due to her accident in July 2013, and passed away on November 17th 2013. She would often say that Fran was with us and talked to her as if she were there. Fran would respond by providing a tiny bright white feather when Benda was around.

I would take Topaz, our dog for a walk over the field and would often get white feathers float down when there was no-one else around. Sometimes I would think about Fran whilst driving to an appointment feeling sad in the car, when a white feather would just appear on the windscreen wiper, or often float past at waist level on the motorway.

The most surprising event though was on Good Friday I think in 2013 when I was sitting down reading the paper around 6pm. It was a cloudy nondescript day but it was April 19th- Fran's birthday. Kay suddenly said what's that outside? I thought it was a few birds flying past but several feathers floated down. We rushed outside and saw a whole bucket load of feathers float down and land around the car in the front drive, which was a most fascinating sight. It was her way for saying 'thank you' for all that we did for her, apparently as we put a card in her room and happy birthday banner which it seems she was aware of.

Obviously life since Fran departed continues, although the house is much quieter now with just the two of us and Topaz here now. The boys have left home and now live with their wives and girlfriends, and no doubt we hope to have grandchildren one day, who will ask about Fran and her life, and we can tell them she was one utterly amazing person who fought an incurable condition that led to her untimely demise. That was a loss not just for her family, but her whole community.

We continue to change the flowers on her grave regularly, and tend to the plants and solar light, as Fran was very much into recycling and ambient energies like me, but Kay believes in the hereafter but not alternative energies necessarily. The plants on her grave have grown enormous, with a large red palm and other bushes flowering splendidly.

Our Aunt Gilly assures us that Fran is safe with both Brenda and Colin now upstairs with her, looking after her. We hope to join her one day when our time down here is done. I often sit by her grave and say that she really shouldn't be there. She should have been at University, travelling the rest of the world she started exploring and having a career. However Fran was not the marrying type and I didn't see myself giving her a wedding speech anytime soon, or her having kids.

Instead I would quietly sit on the bench near her grave and contemplate all the new graves that have appeared since 2009, some of them young people just like Fran, and think she is not alone in this. Of every 1000 girls who start secondary school, statistically only around 996 will finish it alive. It's just a real shame that Fran was one of the 4 in a thousand.

However, I console myself in knowing that since her passing, I see other girls her age and think that there is no-one who even comes close to her or what she achieved in such a brief time. I think of Paloma Faith's 'Only Love can hurt like this' as Fran and I had an almost telepathic relationship. I didn't even need to talk to her to know what she was thinking. I only had that with one other person which was Brother Mike around the age of 18, but that has long gone.

Now I just sit on the bench after tending her grave, as I also have to tend Brenda's and Colin's grave in Potters Bar and my grandparents' grave in Enfield, as no one else seems to bother these days, which is a sad commentary on our society these days. It makes me fear for what will happen when the current generation of older grave tenders are no longer here. Who will look after their graves in the future? Or will they just be simply forgotten, neglected, and overgrown like all too many these days. It is also sad that some 6 years after Fran's death the world has moved on, but not necessarily for the better in some cases.

It seems unfair that one side of the family has been decimated by loss, whilst the other families seem relatively unscathed. However my 18 year association with Fran was unforgettable, and I often think that State One and 'Forever and day' should be her song. When we hear Snow Patrol and 'Chasing cars' on the radio, then we know she is with us spiritually and she comes in often when I am listening to my i-pod as Fran loved 'indie' music. Kay says that her mum Brenda is around when we hear Phil Collins on the radio, and it is her way of letting us know her presence.

For the time being we know Fran is upstairs but still seeking healing from what happened, so it must have been traumatic for her as well as us? That's not something you often realise when someone takes their own life, and the concept that healing can continue even after death is an interesting one. One day I may try regression therapy, as it seems many of us have lived past lives, and are passing through this world before returning to the spirit world.

However for 18 years we had something really special, despite her Asperger's and so it proved to be. I would rather have had 18 unforgettable years than 80 miserable ones though. Wouldn't you?

My Wonderful Fran: Discography

Tracks that Fran liked, bought, or would have approved.

ARTIST	TITLE	SCENE
Colin Mold	Pursuit of Amphibilous	Introduction
Andreas Johnssen	Glorius	Early years
Delirious	Hands of Kindness	Learning to swim
Los Del Rio	The Maccarena	Bay of Naples, age 7
TATU	All the things she said	Archery, age 11
Vanessa Carlton	1000 miles	Cycling down the M1
Metric	Breathing Underwater	Swimming marathon
Snow Patrol	Just say Yes	Youth Talk
Sunskreem v push	Please save me	Jogging at night
Yes	Parallels	Niagara Falls
Colin Mold	Prayer and shelter	Moraine Lake, Canada

Colin Mold	From the spring, hope	Paragliding, Interlaken
Feeder	Feel the moment	Redbourn festival
Bon Jovi	It's my life	Alton Towers
30 Seconds to Mars	Stranger in a strange land	Major Psychotic attack
The Script	Never seen anything	NYE party 2008
Delirious	Obsession	'A' level homework
Savage garden	Crash and burn	Mobile frustration
Nickelback	Gotta be somebody	Darren Brown show
Pink Floyd	Comfortably numb	Fran's death
Snow patrol	Chasing cars	Fran's funeral
Paloma Faith	Only love can hurt	In the cemetery
The Script	Hall of Fame	Presentations/ trophies
State 1	Forever and a day	Finale

About the Author:

Paul Spelzini is fifty-nine at the time of authoring this book, and married 31 years with three children, including Fran who died; and a sheepdog Topaz who is now twelve. Paul is a qualified Chartered Surveyor and Building Engineer by training, with 41 years' of experience in the Construction and Real Estate Industries.

He is a voluntary station adopter with the Abbey Line Community rail partnership since its inception in 2005; and has run a voluntary local transport user group since 1986, campaigning for improvements and saving services that would otherwise have been lost.

He is also a leading UK flight and traditional archer, having had a number of successes over the years, since taking up the sport originally as a target archer in 1998 and switching around 2005.

Paul wrote 'My Wonderful Fran' originally as a biography and record of Fran's life, but felt it could also help other families struggling with ASF, schizophrenia and other related mental illnesses.

END.

Printed in Great Britain
by Amazon

22143347R00076